MW01484839

Divorce Thru the Eyes of a Teen

Activity Guide

Krista Smith

All scriptural references have been taken from the New International Version (NIV) of the Bible, which is published by Zondervan Corporation, Grand Rapids, Michigan (parent company: Harper-Collins Publishers, New York). Used by permission. All rights reserved.

Typeset design by Jane Tokar

Copyright © 2007, 2010 by Krista Smith. All rights reserved.

No part of this publication may be reproduced, transmitted, transcribed, stored in a retrieval system, or translated into any language, in any form or by any means, electronic, mechanical, or otherwise, without prior written permission from the author. No copy or reproduction shall be made, in whole or in part, without the express permission in writing from the author except as provided by USA copyright law.

This curriculum is not intended to be used as a replacement for psychologists or other healthcare professionals. It is designed to be an additional resource to assist in the healing process. If further help is needed, please refer individuals to a psychologist or healthcare professional.

Any products or companies mentioned herein, whether or not accompanied by a trademark, registered trademark, or service mark, are the properties of their respective companies.

Printed in the United States of America.

Publishing services by AMFM Press, Arizona. The views expressed or implied in this work do not necessarily reflect those of AMFM Publishing.

ISBN: 978-0-9796620-3-4

TABLE OF CONTENTS

AMERICAN IDOL

As a fun event during the Weekend Event, you can hold your own unofficial American Idol contest. This is an activity based on the popular T.V. show American Idol. You will need to find your own "Paula", "Simon", "Randy" or "Ryan". Hand out a skit (see skits on page 29) to each team and give them time to work on them as a group. When ready, have everyone come back together, and introduce your own famous judges. At that point, each group has an opportunity to present their skit. When they are finished performing, the judges have an opportunity to "judge" them. There are certain rules you need to convey to your judges—they cannot make fun of any person or group, they cannot talk negatively about any group and they cannot compare one group to another group. The purpose of the judges is to have fun with the contestants by making good, clean comments. If you select a winner, base it on: group members participation, presentation of their topic, and creativity. It is sure to be a riot!

ANGER CUPS

Place three cups upside down with a small object hidden under each. Quickly shuffle the cups with the objects underneath and have the teens try to guess where each object is hidden.

Nugget of Truth: After you play for awhile, explain to them that anger, just like the cup, is usually caused by something deeper, like the object in the cup. In order to handle your anger well, it helps to be able to find out what is underneath that is causing it. For example: Sometimes it can be disappointment; maybe your dad was suppose to pick you up and didn't show. You would be very disappointed but it would come out as anger when you respond by running up to your room and slamming your door and cranking up the music. In order to deal with your anger, you have to acknowledge the disappointment that is hiding "under the cup". Maybe fear is under your anger. Maybe sadness. Maybe hurt. It could be many different things. Either way, spend some time thinking about what is "under the cup" for you.

ANGER THERMOMETER

See attachment section

Make copies of the large thermometer (see attachments). Hand out a thermometer to each teen and have them rate themselves on the thermometer based on how angry they are; tonight, this week, last week etc.

Nugget of Truth – Talk about things that make their thermometers rise and ways they can cool it down again.

BALLOON BALANCE

Give each teen an inflated balloon. Tell them to try to balance it on one finger. Their finger must have contact with the balloon at all times (you can't tap it to keep it in the air). Who can balance the balloon the longest? Have everyone count how long they can keep the balloon balanced on their finger. Make a big deal about how hard it is to keep it on your finger.

Nugget of Truth – It will be very difficult to keep the balloon balanced on your finger. Balancing your emotions at a time like this can be just as hard as balancing the balloon on your finger. No one expects you to get it right every time – neither does God. But by doing your best, it'll come easier each time.

-submitted by Kristen T. Heaney

BEFORE & AFTER

On a white board draw a long line from left to right with "me" on one side and "God" on the other. Have each teen come up to the board one by one and write a "B" on the line for how close they felt to God before the divorce and an "N" for how close they feel to God now. When everyone has had a turn, look at how much everyone has grown through their pain.

Nugget of Truth – Talk about how it is normal for divorce or any changes to affect your relationship with God. Celebrate with them the progress they have made.

-submitted by Kristen T. Heaney

BIG D CANDY

See attachment section

This is a great way to start each session during the weekend format. It works as a great tool to encourage your teens to open up and share their personal experiences in front of the group. Before the weekend, cut up the questions from the Attachment Section and string a piece of ribbon through them. Purchase candy bars or candy (like M&M's, Starbursts, Nerd Ropes etc.) and punch a hole in the wrapper. Tie the ribbon with the attached question around the candy. Prepare a variety of candy questions and place them in a basket. Encourage 2 or 3 teens at the beginning of every session to come up front and pick out a candy bar or candy. Let them know that in order to be able to keep the candy they need to stand up front, read the question and answer it out loud. This is a great way to get a quiet group to open up and it will help them feel more comfortable when sharing in their small groups.

See attachment section

BIG D QUOTES

Sometimes it is helpful for teens to relate to one another by relating to others thoughts and experiences. In the Attachment Section are quotes from various teens sharing how they dealt with their parent's separation and divorce. Type the attached quotes onto 8 1/2 x 11 inch card stock and post them on the walls around the room. Use the quotes as a way for teens to realize they are not alone. These can stay up the entire weekend or for the duration of your weekly session.

BIG D BINGO

See attachment section

This is a great mixer to encourage teens to get to know one another, break the silence, and realize they are not the only one experiencing separation or divorce in their family. Make copies of The Big D Bingo sheet (see attachments) and hand one out to each teen. Encourage them to go around and find people who identify with a square and have them sign in the appropriate box until they get a Bingo or all their squares are filled. Give them 15 to 20 minutes to see how many squares they can fill. Either the first person or every person who comes back with a Bingo wins a prize (candy bar or some small item).

Rule: Only one person can sign one square per Bingo sheet.

BLINDFOLDED SHOE SHUFFLE

Arrange enough chairs in a circle, one for each teen. Have each teen take off their shoes and sit in a chair. Blindfold everyone and put all their shoes in the middle (be sure to mix them up). When you say "go" have them try to find their own shoes, put them back on, while being blindfolded and sit back in a chair. The first person to get back to a chair with their correct shoes on wins. Perhaps you can have a small prize for the winner. Shoes do not have to be tied or buckled, but must be their own and fully on their feet. You can continue as long as you want.

Nugget of Truth – Explain that just like our shoes, our emotions can feel all mixed up during a divorce. And just like our goal in the game was to sort out the shoes, our goal at "The Big D" is to help you sort out your feelings.

-submitted by Kristen T. Heaney

BLUEFISH TV

See attachment section

One of the best ways to get teens to feel comfortable is to help them identify with someone else their age. There are some awesome video clips available online. Go to www.bluefishtv.com and search under "teens and divorce". There you will find a variety of video clips of teens sharing their experiences of how they dealt with their parents divorce. You can request a copy of the DVD from my website to use in your ministry or you can download them yourself. The videos on the DVD from my website are listed in the Attachment Section.

See attachment section

BOUNDARIES

Make copies of the picket fence (see attachments) for each participant. Hand out the fence worksheet to every teen and ask them to think of situations in their life where they need to set up a boundary to promote safety and healing. Ask them to write or draw the situations on the fence. It is important for them to first recognize the need for a boundary, then set the boundary, making sure it is fair to all involved. For example, I will not be a part of bad mouthing my other parent with my mom or dad. And when it begins to happen, I will tell them that I wish they wouldn't talk about my other parent in that way or I will leave the room.

BUILD ME UP NOTE CARD

Hand out a note card to each teen. Have them write the name and something positive about the person on their left. Then pass it to the right. Repeat this process until the cards make it around the circle. At the end of the session hand out the cards to the appropriate people. This is a great exercise to build each others self-esteem.

CENTERPIECE TREASURE BOX

This is something you can do at the Weekend Event to add to each session as a reminder of what was learned. Wrap a box with a cover for every table. As you start each session pull out something that symbolizes that topic. Hand one out to everyone to put in their own Big D Bag to take home as a reminder of what they learned. Below are some suggestions –

    Stepping Stones to Healing – a stone (they can write on the stone which step they think they are on)

    Anger – a stress ball

    Hurt – a band aid

    Single Parent Home – a slinky (being pulled in 2 different directions)

    Blended Family Home – a puzzle piece or mini puzzle

    Forgiveness – White Out or an eraser

    Acceptance – a journal

CHAINS OF HOPE

See attachment section

Prior to the session, cut up strips of colored paper. Place them in a pile in the middle of the table. Ask the teens to write on the strips of paper things they have learned and ways they have changed for the better since attending "The Big D". Leaders are encouraged to participate too. If they want to share what they are writing, they may, but it is not required. When everyone has written at least one thing take the strips of paper and form links and then chain their links together to form a long chain. Hang this in your room as a testimony of the work that has been done since "The Big D" began. This also makes a great gift to share with the pastoral staff of your church.

-submitted by Kristen T. Heaney

CHOICES

Bring a couple of different snacks each night and give everyone the chance to choose which snack they want. An apple or an orange, pretzels or peanut butter sandwiches. This is a great way to demonstrate the ability and freedom to make choices at a time in their life when it may feel like they have no choices. Let them rejoice in the small choices.

COMFORT CARDS

See attachment section

Beforehand copy the Comfort Cards (see attachments) on card stock and cut them out. When you are sharing about God's comfort even in the midst of their pain, offer them encouragement by handing out these Comfort Cards. Suggest they keep these verses with them so when they need to be reminded they are loved and that God is with them, they can pull these cards out, read them, and find strength and encouragement through them.

COMFORT ZONE

It is very important that you continuously remind everyone that this is their "Comfort Zone". They need to know that whatever is shared when you are together is confidential between only you and them. It is vital that trust is developed and maintained. The only exception to this rule is if you discover abuse that is happening or if you are seriously concerned for someone's safety. In those cases you need to report it to the proper authorities. But other than that, confidentiality and comfort is one of the most important things you can give these teens. By experiencing trust they will be freer to open up and learn to trust others again.

COMMUNICATION 101

Prior to this session bring a fishing pole and remove the hook or you can make a "fishing pole" out of a stick and fishing line for each small group. Purchase a few bagels and tie one on the end of each fishing line. This activity is a relay, so have each group participate at the same time. Have each small group select a Listener, a Communicator, and a Receiver. Have someone tie a blindfold on each Listener and Receiver. Have the Listener kneel on a chair and ask the Receiver to lie down on the floor with their head directly below the Listener. When you say go hand the Listener a fishing pole with bagel attached and tell the Communicator to explain to the Listener how to move the pole in order for the Receiver to be able to bite into the bagel. The Receiver has to keep their head on the floor and can't use their hands. The first group who can catch the bagel in their mouth wins.

Nugget of Truth: Talk about the importance to speak clearly and thoroughly when communicating with others. If you do not take the time to make sure you have Been understood, things will continue to be confusing and frustrating for everyone. Remember the clearer you communicate, the better chance you will be heard and start making progress.

EMOTION CHARADES

See attachment section

This is played like normal charades but it involves emotions instead of objects. On small slips of paper write some emotions that teens could act out, like anger, happy, sad, scared, annoyed, surprised, excited, disgusted, jealous, impatient, shame etc. You can find a list of various emotions under Feelings Words in the Attachment Section. Ask for volunteers to come up, pick an emotion and act it out as the rest of the group tries to figure out what the emotion is.

Nugget of Truth: After everyone has done a charade, share how difficult it is to convey your feelings or pick up on how others are feelings just by actions alone. This is why it is so important to effectively communicate how you are feeling. You can't assume your parents or anyone else knows exactly how you are feeling unless you tell them yourself.

-Submitted by Kristen T. Heaney

See attachment section

FAMILY CHAIR GAME

Before your teens arrive, set up a circle of chairs. When you are ready to begin, have everyone sit in a chair. Once everyone is seated remove any extra chairs. Read the statements from the Attachment Section, one by one. If the statement applies to them, instruct the students to move in the direction and the amount of chairs read. If someone is in that chair, they need to share the chair, sit on a lap, or stand behind that chair. This will hopefully turn into pandemonium as people are stacked 5 high with someone needing to get up from the bottom. The purpose of the game is to be a mixer, have fun, and emphasize that no family is the same. It doesn't matter what your family looks like, we may all have different backgrounds but we are still a family. Be creative and add more statements of your own.

Nugget of Truth: After you have played for awhile, share that we all come from different types of families. No two families are alike, every family has its unique and special qualities. It is important not to compare your family to others and wish it were different. We need to learn to accept our families for who and what they are and learn to work together, not against each other.

FAMILY CHANGE GAME

See attachment section

Before teens arrive prepare a bowl filled with whatever kind of candy you brought (m&m's, skittles, jelly beans) per table. Have enough small paper cups for everyone to have one. Once it is time to start, hand out the paper cups and put the bowl of candy in the center of each table. As you are doing this ask everyone to go and wash their hands. When ready have everyone put five pieces of candy into each of their cups. As you read the questions from the Attachment Section, for every statement that applies to them they are to do what it says. Continue as long as you want. Be creative and add more statements of your own. When you are finished, they are free to eat the candy.

Variation - A prize can be given to the person who ended up with the most candy indicating they have experienced the most changes and are still hanging in there.

FATHERS LOVE LETTER

Go to www.fathersloveletter.com to download an incredible love letter written from God, our heavenly Father to us, His sons and daughters. There are many different download options available including ones with music, ones based solely on Scriptures and many more. It is an amazing way to share God's love in a way they are sure to never forget.

See attachment section

FEELINGS ACTIVITY BOX

Put together a "Feelings Box" at home (see attachments) and bring it with you. Hand out all the items from the box to those in the room. When all items have been distributed, read the scenarios from the Attachment Section and ask them to explain how they could use their particular item to help them process their feelings.

FEELINGS ALPHABET RACE

See attachment section

This is a fun and easy mixer. Beforehand place a white board in front of the room and list the alphabet from A to Z. Hand out a Feelings Alphabet Race worksheet (see attachments) to everyone. Explain that you will give them 3 minutes to think of any feeling that starts with each letter of the alphabet. After three minutes have everyone share feelings they came up with for each letter and write them down on the white board. Write their feeling beside the appropriate letter (A-anger, J-joy). This is a great way to get their minds thinking about different feelings and can be used as a reference point throughout the session.

Option: You can hand out a small prize to the person who comes up with the most feelings in 3 minutes.

Leaders Note: In the Attachment Section there is an extensive list of feelings in case you get stuck on one letter.

Variation - After all the feelings are listed, go back over the list and decide, as a group, which feelings are examples of positive feelings and which ones are negative. Remember, some can be both, depending on how it is communicated.

FEELINGS BALLS

Ahead of time, you will need to purchase tennis balls. On each ball write a feeling; for example: fear, anger depressed, guilt, irritated, worried, anxious, disappointed etc. Have everyone stand in a circle and give a ball to someone in the circle and have them say what the feeling is as they toss it to someone else in the circle. After a couple of times, when it seems like they understand, add another ball with a different feeling on it. Be sure each time they pass the ball, they read the feeling on the ball before they toss it. Keep adding balls until all the balls are active in the circle and things start getting chaotic as balls are flying everywhere and different feelings are being repeated quickly. Notice how overwhelmed the teens are getting. Now start taking the balls away one by one. When you get back to one ball
explain that we experience many emotions throughout a week, a day or sometimes an hour. Talk about how much more chaotic the game became with the addition of another emotion. Remind the teens that it is usually healthier for us if we can deal with just one or two emotions at a time rather than trying to juggle several at once.

Nugget of Truth: Share with them that when your family is going through a divorce your emotions may feel this way. You may have many different feelings at many different times and it will most likely feel overwhelmed much of the time. As you deal with your feelings one by one your life will start feeling less crazy again.
-Submitted by: Kristen T. Heaney

Variation – Instead of you preparing the feelings balls, bring in the balls and have each teen label their own ball with their own feeling. When they are done labeling their own ball, stand in a circle and have them start by saying their feeling and then tossing their ball to someone else. As soon as a ball is tossed to them, they have to look at the ball and say the feeling before they can toss it to someone else. Keep on going until there are balls everywhere and no one can keep up. As balls start falling, start taking them away one by one. Help them to notice that as you remove some balls it gets less overwhelming.

Nugget of Truth: Explain to them that this is the way it is in life sometimes, especially during a separation or divorce. You can have so many feelings and at times you just can't handle it all. At times like that it is easier to remove them one by one by dealing with them. And soon you will not feel as overwhelmed and be able to handle things better again. What's important is that you recognize when you need to start dealing with your feelings because you can't keep them all inside forever. The more you are honest and deal with them the better off you will be.

FEELINGS CENTERPIECE

See attachment section

As a way of encouraging your teens to recognize and acknowledge feelings they are experiencing, try taping a piece of paper on the center of their tables with the word "feelings" faded in the background. You can also use the sheet in the Attachment Section as a placemat for everyone. Encourage them to jot or doodle any feelings they may be experiencing throughout the sessions. We suggest you don't spend any time analyzing these feelings, just use this as a tool to help them recognize and label feelings as they feel them. Sometimes teens tend to listen better when doodling as well.

FIRE, WATER AND ICE

For this exercise, you will need matches, two pitchers of water, a block of ice, and a tarp for under the table. Start this activity by telling the kids that after the demonstration they will be able to come up and touch some of the props you will be using, but while you are talking they will be expected to sit and listen. Explain to them that in order to learn how to respond to anger in a healthy way, you have to know the difference between fire, water and ice.

- FIRE – Explain to them as you strike a match, "When you are feeling intense feelings of anger, you're too "hot" to process the anger and should wait until you "cool down". Reacting to anger while you are still "on fire" usually gets you into trouble".
- WATER – As you pour water gently from one pitcher to another and back again, say, "You want to wait until you have cooled down to "water". Water has enough force to create electricity when it is controlled properly and, over time, can carve through mountains with a gentle stream. The water still has great power and effect, but it is not too intense. If we manage our anger like water, we will be able to respond in a healthy way".
- ICE – Start chiseling on the block of ice and say, "This ice is difficult to break through. Even if there was something in the center of it, we would have trouble picking through to find it. The ice represents how our hearts can turn if we hold on to our anger for too long with out expressing it. Anger that we don't face, turns our hearts as cold as ice and is very unhealthy for us".

Nugget of Truth: When we are angry at someone or about something, we can sometimes react like the fire...too quickly, before we've thought it through. Or sometimes, we wait too long and just stuff our anger and become like blocks of ice. But, with God's help, we can be like the water – people who express their anger in healthy ways and continue to flow into the healthy people God created us to be. Are you Fire, Water, or Ice today? How will you choose to handle your anger – like Fire, Water or Ice?

- submitted by: Kristen T. Heaney

GAME HOST

This works best when used within the weekend format. It is a great help to have a designated "Game Host" who handles all of the games and mixers. Your Game Host can also be your MC for the weekend and take care of introducing all the games, managing the chaos, and keeping things on schedule. This also gives the leader a much needed break in between sessions.

See attachment section

GET OFF MY BACK

Before group begins, write a feeling word (examples are listed under Feeling Words in the attachments) on a label for every teen or use a 3 x 5 card and place a piece of double sided tape on the back. As each teen arrives put the card or label (that they have not seen) on their back. If the tape does not stick use a pin to attach it to the back of their shirt. Tell them they have to guess what feeling is written on their back by asking other people questions or by having people act it out as they try to guess.

Rule: They can only ask "Yes" or "No" questions or silently act it out.

Examples of feelings you could use: Depressed, Lonely, Relieved, Scared, Abandoned, Aching, Aggravated, Alone, Anxious, Conflicted, Bitter, Bruised, Burdened, etc. See attachments for more suggestions. After some time, go around the room and ask everyone what they think their feeling is.

GRADUATION

If time permits, holding a Graduation Ceremony for those who have participated in "The Big D" is a great way of recognizing their commitment and acknowledging the work they have put into their healing process. It is important to invite their parents so they can also recognize them for the commitment they have shown. Make a special effort to invite both parents if possible. To add an extra touch send out invitations to the participants and their parents. A suggestion could be to have a pizza party, a potluck or a picnic. Keep in mind that mixing both parents together in the same room may be a little uncomfortable so be intent on keeping it light and comfortable. It is great to spend some time sharing with the parents some of the things you have done over the past weeks, without giving out any personal information. The most important thing is to take time during the night to specifically recognize each and every student by name and share what you have appreciated about them. This is a very meaningful experience and something the teens will never forget. It is a great way to end your time together.

HANGMAN

See attachment section

This uses the same phrases as Wheel of Fortune (see attachments) but is played like Hang Man instead. It is a great way to switch things up after you have done a few groups.

-submitted by Robyn Besemann

HIDDEN GIFT GAME

This game is like a white elephant gift exchange. During the week purchase a number of gifts ranging in all shapes and sizes. The Dollar Store is a good place to find some good, silly, strange gifts. Don't forget to wrap them. Have the kids choose a number from 1 to the number of kids you have present. The teen with the number 1 chooses a wrapped gift and sits back in his/her seat. The teen with # 2 may either choose to steal # 1's gift or choose another from the pile. Of course, this is a risk, because # 1's gift is still not revealed. Really emphasize the *choice* in the matter. Say things like, "What will you choose?" "What a difficult choice!"

This goes on until the last person chooses a gift. Then everyone can unwrap their gifts. They will find it hilarious when the gift they all fought over was really a bar of soap disguised in a bigger box or a roll of toilet paper or the gift no one wanted was bag of candy.

Nugget of Truth: Wrap up discussion by telling them that sometimes in life the choices you need to make can be scary because you don't know what the outcome will be. Remind them that if they trust in God, they can know that in the end, regardless of their life circumstances, He is always on their side and promises to give them hope and a future. At the end you can pass out a small gift to everyone (maybe a chocolate hug kiss).

- *submitted by: Kristen T. Heaney*

HOW TO SAY IT

Give each teen a 3x5" card and ask them to think of someone they are having a hard time communicating with. Ask them to write down what it is they would like to say to that person and read it over a few times. You can even break off into groups of two or three and practice. Encourage them to use "I feel" statements instead of "you" statements. Suggest they take it home and practice reading it a few more times over the next couple of days and look for a time when they can share their feelings with that particular person. This will help them to feel more confident and comfortable sharing their thoughts and feelings when the opportunity arises.

See attachment section

HURTS BANDAIDS CAN'T COVER

This activity encourages teens to consider their hurts, worries and fears, and give them an opportunity to share what they have been struggling with. Beforehand, you need to prepare a large red heart and cut a zigzag through it like a broken heart and put it up on the wall. You also need to copy and cut out plenty of the band-aids (see attachments). Make sure you have plenty of thumb tacks or tape and pens. Place enough band-aids on the tables so every person has enough for at least six each, but don't specifically hand six to each person. Play some soft soothing Christian music in the background (see Reflective Songs in Attachment Section).

Start by saying something like:
We all have many hurts that have affected us by our parent's choice to separate or divorce. Many times these hurts were not caused by us and we have no control over stopping them. The hard thing about these hurts is that there is no quick fix. Whatever it is that has caused pain in your life, it hurts very bad. We were taught when we were young that band-aids cured everything. When we fell and got hurt, we would run to our mom or dad and they would give it a kiss and put a band-aid on it, it was so easy then. But divorce is not a minor scrape that heals quickly. These hurts cannot be healed by simply putting a band-aid on it. These hurts go deep and we may think that we will never be okay again. On every table there are some band-aids. Spend some time thinking about different hurts, worries, or fears that you have experienced. Write them on the band-aids that are in front of you. When you feel ready you can come up and pin or tape them on the broken heart.

Leaders Note – to get things started you may want to read some of the suggestions in the Attachment Section. It is also suggested to save the band aids to use again when doing the "Take it to the Cross" activity on page 31.

IN THEIR SHOES

See attachment section

This is a great activity to help everyone consider how other people in their family may view the same situation but from a different point of view. Place a set of footprints (see attachments) on the floor. Copy and cut each separate situation in the Attachment Section. Have the teens read out loud the examples and share how they would feel in each situation, if they were "in the other persons shoes". Take a look at each situation from different points of view. The best time to do this activity is when you are talking about blended families.

See attachment section

Variation: You can use an old pair of boots or shoes (large enough for teens to slip their feet in and out of) instead of the set of footprints.

Nugget of Truth: See how changing your perspective can help you understand difficult situations better if you take the time to look at it through their eyes as well. You may even discover finding other positive aspects that you may not have seen before.

JESUS BAGS

The idea of this activity is to encourage teens to think about who they are vs. how they think others see them. Hand out a lunch size paper bag to everyone and have a lot of miscellaneous magazines out on the tables. Start by explaining to them to envision the bag as representing themselves. As they look through the magazines cut out and glue pictures or words onto their bag that illustrate who they are. Ask them to decorate the outside of their bag with things that describe who they are on the outside. Make sure they label their bags with their names too. Then tell them you want them to take a deeper look at who they are on the inside and go through the magazines and cut out things they think describe who they are on the inside as well and place them inside their bags. This could be feelings they feel, close relationships they have, fears they feel, secrets they hold, thoughts they have, struggles they experience, people they trust, etc. We suggest that you play soft music in the background (see Reflective Songs in the attachment section).

After you let them decorate their bags, put the Jesus Hearts (see attachments) on the tables. This would be a great time to share your Salvation Story. As they color or decorate their Jesus Heart, invite those who have Christ in their lives to put their Jesus Heart into their bag. Be careful not to assume everyone has accepted Christ. Let them know that if they have not accepted Christ in their heart, they can do it today.

When the bags are completed, take time to let everyone explain who they are through the bags they created. Make sure everyone is accepted for whoever they are and they know that Christ died specifically for each one of them. This is a good activity to use near the beginning of your time together. If you have too many bags to share in one night, you can spread them out throughout the next few weeks.

LETTERS

See attachment section

At any time throughout your sessions, you can encourage your teens to write letters to God, their Mom and/or their Dad. You can make copies from the sample letters in the Attachment Section. If you decide to do this during group, you may want to play some soft music in the background (see Reflective Songs in the Attachment Section).

LIGHTBULB MOMENT

See attachment section

This is a great activity to do towards the end of your sessions. Beforehand, make copies of the large light bulb (see attachments). Hand out a light bulb worksheet to every teen. Ask them to think back to all the different sessions and write in the light bulb different "Aha" moments they experienced while attending "The Big D". When finished, have them share things they have learned with one another. You can display them on the walls or share them with your pastoral team.

-submitted my Kristen T. Heaney

M & M or SKITTLE

This is a great activity to use during the Change sessions. Prior to the session, purchase fun size bags of *M & M's and Skittles.* Hand out the M&M's to those currently living in a Single Parent home and the Skittles to those living in a step-family home. Ask them not to open their bag of candy until you give them instructions. After everyone has a bag of candy, go around the room and have them open their candy and share things that have changed about their new home, whether single parent or step-family, for each piece of candy in their bag. It can be things they like or dislike about the change. They can eat the candy once they have shared.

Leaders Note: If their parents are "separated" but still living under the same roof, consider them to be living in a single parent home because emotionally they are. If they have one parent single and one remarried, they should choose whichever home they want to use.

MORE THAN A SHADOW

This is a great activity to build their self esteem. It is also a great team building exercise. You will need a projector and white paper. Tape the paper on the wall, then have each teen, one at a time, stand between the projector and paper and have a leader trace their silhouette from their shoulders up. After their silhouette is drawn, pass them around the room and have everyone write at least one positive comment about the person inside their shadow. When everyone has finished writing (leaders too) give each teen their own silhouette to bring home or put them up on the wall.

-submitted by: Kristen T. Heaney

MOVIE CLIPS

Topic: Not wanting to be here but it is best for them right now.

Movie – 28 Days

...any scene with Sandra Bullock's struggle with wanting to leave rehab.

Topic: Mixed feelings

Movie – Shrek

...any scene where donkey is confused and has all kinds of mixed emotions.

Topic: Self Esteem

Movie – Hope Floats

Start: 126:00   Stops: 131:10

...scene after Bernie visits dad in the Nursing Home. Clip ends after Grandma and Bernie's talk. Reinforce the notion that family can be your hope...even though the definition of your family is changing right now. Allow others to help you and work towards healing from the divorce.

Topic: Hope

Movie – Count of Monte Cristo

Chapter 10-37:40 and end after Dantes' asks "When do we start?"

...in this scene, Dantes has been in prison for 7 years and has lost all hope. Another inmate, a priest, emerges into Dantes cell from a hole that the priest has been digging with hopes of escape. This scene shows how hope can emerge – note the change in Dantes hope from the start of the clip to the end.

Topic: Forgiveness

Movie – Home Again

...scene at the end with Kevin and the old man in the church.

Topic: Anger

Movie – Water Boy

Starts: 13:08   Stops: 15:22

...in the movie the water boy of a football team becomes the star and gets the girl after he finds a way to channel his anger for a positive purpose and outcome. Bobby learns to channel his anger in another way. When the team teases Bobby it triggers some childhood memories and Bobbie lets out his anger by tackling a football player on the field. As the story proceeds, Bobby ends up becoming the star on his team when he channels his anger in the right direction. This movie illustrates the power of anger, both for good and bad.

Topic: Communication

Movie – Anywhere But Here

Start: 123:42   Stops: 127:19

...Natalie Portman finally makes a call to her dad who left when she was very young. She wants to have a relationship with him but has trouble expressing this to him when she senses that he is only interested in sending her money. Discussion – how do you think she felt after this conversation? What could she have done differently to get a better outcome from this phone conversation? (maybe planned her words out prior, imagines the possibility of his negative reaction and what her response might be, instead of hanging up she could have told him how disappointed she was that she did not have an active father, she could have listened to him more and not assumed how he was feeling.)

Topic: Change

Movie – Pay It Forward

...You can make change, you can have an impact. This boy chose to have a positive impact. What impact will you make on this world – do you realize what a huge impact you can have? Don't let this divorce be an excuse for you to extinguish the light you can be to this world.

Illustration – Light one candle in a darkened room during discussion then extinguish.

NOT MY FAULT

This activity should be done as a group activity. It emphasizes that it is not their fault that their parents have separated. Their parents have made choices that affect their lives and those choices had nothing to do with what they did or did not do. It is a fun activity that will promote teamwork and has a clear meaning at the end.

Form two teams or if you have enough teens break up into teams of 3 or 4 and give them each a puzzle to put together. Bring an easy kids puzzle (15 pcs or so) with some similar looking pieces from another puzzle mixed in. If you are using 2 or 3 different puzzles you can put a few pieces from the other puzzles in each of the boxes. Ask the kids to put the puzzles together. They will obviously have a hard time completing the puzzles because not all the pieces belong to the same puzzle. Push them along by saying, "Come on, this is a little kid's puzzle, you should be done by now" etc. After they have struggled for awhile, stop the group and say, "Oh, wait...It's not your fault! It's my fault that you can't do the puzzle because I switched the pieces on you. Some of the pieces are from a different puzzle and they don't fit. It's not your fault."

Nugget of Truth: Explain to them that we are like this, puzzles that could not be finished because since the separation or divorce pieces of their lives don't seem to fit anymore and it is not their fault. It can be frustrating to arrange the pieces of your life after divorce...but it's important to remember that divorce is not your fault. Just like you didn't do anything wrong when you couldn't get the puzzle together, you did not do anything to cause your parents divorce. Divorce is a choice made by parents, because of choices parents make, not because of anything you or your siblings might have done or not done. Have everyone around the tables say out loud "It's Not My Fault".

- submitted by: Kristen T. Heaney

OPTICAL ILLUSIONS

See attachment section

Hand out the Optical Illusions (see attachments) and go over each one with the group.
Ask them these questions for each picture:
1. Do you see the words "Optical Illusion"?
2. Can you count the black dots?
3. Are the horizontal lines parallel or do they slope?
4. How many legs does the elephant have?
5. Do you see a rabbit or a duck?
6. Do you see a man playing a horn or a woman's face?
7. What do you see? A princess or an old woman?
8. Do you see a two or a three pronged fork?
9. Stare at the black dot in the center and move your head forward and back.
10. Do you see a rabbit or a duck?

Nugget of Truth: Emphasize that just like you can see different images in these pictures there is usually always 2 ways to view any situation. If you're looking at a situation negatively, there is probably another way to look at the situation to see a different perspective. Try to learn to look at all the different perspectives before forming an opinion.

PANEL DISCUSSION

This is a great activity to encourage questions and give teens the opportunity to get opinions from a variety of people. Suggested panel participants could include: a single parent, a step parent, a non-custodial parent, a college-aged teen who has experienced divorce in their family, a teen their age, a blended family teen and possibly a blended family parent who came into the family without kids of their own. It is a good idea to promote this event to the teens a few weeks prior by having a confidential place for them to leave questions they may want to ask. You will also need an MC (see Game Host on page 15) to field the questions and keep things moving. It is a good idea to have the MC familiarize him or herself with the questions beforehand so they have some time to decide who to pose the questions to. If there are not enough questions you can always have an "open mic" or prepare questions of your own ahead of time.

PAPER CUP FAMILY STRUCTURES

This activity will help the students get to know each other and their family situations better. You will need approximately a dozen Styrofoam cups per person and markers.

Hand out one Styrofoam cup to every person for every person in their immediate family. Hand out markers and have them draw faces and label each cup to identify each member of their family. Encourage them to be creative.

When done, have each teen introduce their family structures using the cups. For instance, Dad and Mom would be on separate sides. Any step parents would be on their parent's side along with any step siblings. Any birth brother and sisters who travel back and forth with them would be included with their (the teen's) cup. If living with friends or grandparents, they can be included too. Pets can be included if wanted. Have them explain how much time is spent at each home as well.

This is a great opportunity to learn more about their family situations. Allow them to describe and share as much about their families as they want. Observe the creative ways they draw each family member and their body language as they explain their family dynamics.

See attachment section

PASS THE FEELING

Make copies of the 4 or 5 (depending on how many groups you may have) different "Pass the Feeling" worksheets from the Attachment Section. While everyone is in their small groups, hand one worksheet out per table. Give each group 3 minutes to come up with as many different things they can for that topic. At the end of 3 minutes, pass the worksheet on to the next table and repeat the process. After every group has had a chance to do each worksheet, collect them all and hand one out to each table. Give each group some more time to work together to analyze the findings.

Were there any similarities between the answers? Did it seem to matter if a guy or girl answered the questions? Were there trends a particular group seemed to follow? Did the age of the group members seem to make a difference with how they answered? Were there statements that seemed to be alike? When finished invite a spokesperson to come forward and share what they came up with.

PICK TWO

See attachment section

Have everyone sit in a circle. Place a number of random objects in the center of the circle (see suggested items in Attachment Section). Go around the room one by one and have everyone choose 2 objects, one that reminds them of who they were before their parents separated and one that reminds them of who they are after their parent's separation or divorce. Once they all have selected two items, go around the circle and take turns describing why they chose the items they did.

PLAYING CARD MIXER

Take a deck of playing cards and mix them up. As you greet the teens when they come have them pick a card – any card. Using an odd sized deck can add a different dimension.

When it is time to start the evening, go around the room and have everyone say something about themselves they haven't shared yet for every number represented on the card.

For example: if you pull an eight, you need to share eight different new things about you.

Variation: Have the red cards (diamond & hearts) represent good or positive things and have the black cards (spades & clubs) represent negative things.

To switch things up a bit you can be more specific and use any topic. Some possibilities may be—things that make you angry, changes since the divorce, hurts you've experienced, positives and negatives about the divorce, things that happened during the week, let your imagination run wild.

Rule: Aces are considered one and Kings, Queens and Jacks are considered ten.

PLUSES & MINUSES

See attachment section

This activity is best done toward the end of the sessions. Hand out the Pluses and Minuses worksheet (see attachments). Encourage everyone to open their minds and take a look at the whole picture. Through "The Big D" you may have discovered that not everything that has happened to you because of the divorce has necessarily been bad. Take a moment and reflect on some of the pluses and minuses that would never have happened without this event in your life. This may help them turn the corner and possibly see some positive things in their lives that have happened since the separation/divorce.

POSITIVE THINKING

Pass out a note card to every teen. On each card ask them to write out Deuteronomy 31:6 (written below) on the back and write their name on the top of the lined side. Then have them pass their card to the person on their right and have that person write something positive about them on it. Continue passing each card to the right until everyone has gotten a chance. Encourage them to take this seriously and monitor what is being written to make sure everyone is writing appropriate comments. When finished have them give the card back to the original owner. Encourage them to bring it home and when they are feeling down, read it, to remind them why they are special.

Be strong and courageous. Do not be afraid or terrified because of them, for the Lord your God goes with you; He will never leave you or forsake you. Deuteronomy 31:6

- Submitted by Kristen Heaney

PRETZEL COMFORT

Have everyone fold their arms across their chests. Now tell them to cross their arms the opposite way – with their other arm on top. Help them recognize how uncomfortable it is.

Nugget of Truth: Explain to them how it's similar to the way we get comfortable with our daily routine, then when change comes, it can feel very uncomfortable.

PURITY AND MARRIAGE SESSION

This is a great opportunity to talk to teens about how their parent's separation and divorce may affect their own personal dating relationships and future spouses. If time allows take an extra week and split the guys and gals in two separate groups and discuss the importance of being more aware of new vulnerabilities that they may experience. Discuss purity and boundary issues. Below are examples of areas you could talk about that are now issues to consider due to the changes in their families.

- Filling an empty hole from an absent father or mother role in your life.
- Extra freedom that comes when your parent is dating as well.
- No good role models-parents living together with boyfriend/girlfriend.
- Too much time home alone (too much idle time usually leads to trouble).
- Looking for love and acceptance, sometimes in all the wrong places.
- List their top 10 qualities they want in their future spouse some day.

Another suggestion is for you to have each teen write up a purity pledge to God. They can come up with some boundaries to hold themselves accountable.
It may be a good idea to find a trusted youth pastor or person who has a passion for teens to present this topic. It can be a sensitive and difficult subject. This session can be used as a great opportunity to get your youth staff involved.

REFLECTIVE SONGS

These are songs you can use during workbook time or times of reflection such as Hurts Bandaids Can't Cover, Letters, Jesus Bags and Take it to the Cross.

I Will Praise You in the Storms–Casting Crowns
Breathe – Michael W. Smith
Better Hands Now – Natalie Grant
Every Season – Nichole Nordeman
I Give You My Heart – Michael W. Smith
God Will Make a Way – Don Moen
Cry Out to Jesus – Third Day
Come to the Rescue – Hillsong United
Come to Jesus – Chris Rice
All I Need is You – Hillsong United

You Are My Hope – Skillet
The Real Me – Natalie Grant
Over My Head – Brian Littrel
Hold Me Jesus – Rich Mullins ·
You Are Everything – Matthew West
Give Me Words to Speak – Aaron Shust
Come My Way – Skillet
East to West – Casting Crowns
I Will Rise—Chris Tomlin
What Faith Can Do—Kutless

SCRIPTURE BALLOON RACE

See attachment section

Write out the words from Philippians 4: 6 & 7 (written below and in the Attachment Section) and cut out each word separately and roll it up. Put the rolled up pieces of paper inside a balloon, blow up the balloon and tie it. When the balloons are blown up with the words inside attach a two foot piece of string on each.

Philippians 4: 6 & 7
Do not be anxious about anything, but in everything, by prayer and petition with thanksgiving, present your requests to God. And the peace of God which transcends all understanding will guard your hearts and minds in Christ Jesus. (NIV)

When you are ready to begin, hand out a balloon with string to each person and have everyone tie them around their ankles. If you do not have enough people for all the balloons, you can give each person two or more balloons. When you say "Go" they need to chase each other around the room trying to pop each others balloons and find the pieces of paper that were hidden inside the balloons. When all the balloons are popped they need to work together to complete the verse. They can use a NIV Bible if they want.

SCRIPTURE PUZZLE RACE

See attachment section

This is a fun way to include scripture with the grief cycle (see Stepping Stones to Healing on page 30). All you need to do is write out the following scriptures onto tag board and cut out each word in the shape of a puzzle piece. Do this for all 5 scriptures. Divide your group into 5 teams and pass out a puzzle to each group and have a race to see who can assemble their puzzle the quickest. When everyone is done, have each team read their scriptures out loud and guess which step it is pertaining to.

- Denial – Romans 15:3 (NIV)
- Anger – Ephesians 4:26-27 (NIV)
- Depression – Proverbs 3:5-6 (NIV)
- Bargaining – Phil. 4:11 (NIV)
- Acceptance – Duet. 28:2 (NIV)

Leaders Note: If you are doing the Weekend Event and are having the Breakouts, this is a great opening activity for each Breakout Session. (see Stepping Stone Stations on page 30)

SCRIPTURE SEARCH GAME

See attachment section

Break into teams of two or more. Make sure each team has a NIV Bible. Hand out the worksheet (in attachment section) to each team and the first team to look up the scriptures, answer the questions and fill in the blanks to complete the puzzle wins. If time allows read the scriptures to discover God's true desire to comfort us. Answers are in the Attachments Section also.

Leaders Note: The answers came from the NIV version.

SKITS

See attachment section

Included in the Attachment Section are a number of skits you can use. There are four actual scripted skits, four stories that can be acted out, and three separate scenes that can be put into your own words. We have used these for American Idol (see American Idol on page 5), leaders have acted them out for examples, or each group has come up with their own skits during the Weekend Event. Use your imagination.

THE SLIPPERY SLOPE BOARD GAME

A new board game created by the author of The Big D designed to help players open up and deal with the feelings and emotions associated with the grief they feel when going through their parents separation or divorce.

Fun for ALL ages—Three different versions—
KIDS—TEENS—ADULTS

Three versions of the game available are:
KIDS—ages 5-12
TEENS—ages 10-19
ADULTS—ages 18+
To order visit www.sonsetpointministries.com.

Great tool to be used in homes or during group sessions.

SLIPPERY SLOPE

See attachment section

Make a copy of the Slippery Slope (see attachments) and after going over the grief cycle have each teen indicate on the slope where they think they are at in their own personal grief cycle. Be sure to discuss that the reason it is called a Slippery Slope is because you never stay at one spot very long and it is very common to slide back and forth throughout the healing journey.

See attachment section

SOLAR SYSTEM

Make copies of the Solar System worksheet (see attachments) and hand one out to every teen. Just like the solar system works interdependently, we work best when we rely on and work together with our own support system. Start by having everyone write their names in the middle on the sun. Then write the names of people in your support system inside the planets circling the sun. To help them create their Solar System ask the following questions:

What adult would you talk to besides your parents if you need to talk?

Who can you depend on? Who is always there for you?

If you ever got into trouble, who would you call for help?

Some suggestions are; coaches, teachers, counselors, pastors, youth leaders etc.

-submitted by: Kristen Heaney

STEPPING STONES

See attachment section

This activity works best when doing the weekend format. You can use it as an additional visual aid when you are reading the quotes from each stage of grief. Bring in some sort of large stone, either real or fake. (It could be as simple as a piece of paper with a stone drawn on it or a paper mache stone.) Have enough leaders to represent the 5 stages of grief. When starting each stage, have a leader portray each stage by acting out the statements in the Attachment Section. As each stone is revealed, have them remain

standing, holding their stones towards the group until all 5 stones are revealed and read out loud. If you do not have that many leaders, you can ask for volunteers from the group.

STEPPING STONE STATIONS

As a way of providing more interaction and movement, you can divide out the Stepping Stones to Healing into 5 different Break Out groups. This is best used during the Weekend Event. You will need 5 different leaders to share on each topic and the teens will move from group to group learning about each stage. You can go through each worksheet in the groups and using the Scripture Puzzle Race is a great way to start out each Break Out.

SURVIVOR ISLAND

This is an awesome creative idea. It is best to be used during the Weekend Event. Building off of the popular "Survivor" TV show you can decorate your room like an island. Have your small groups divide into "tribes" and decorate each table like a hut. We have used umbrella tables and they have worked great. We suggest having a "tribe leader" for each tribe who is preferably college aged and has experienced divorce in their family. To build on the theme we call their small group time "Tribal Counsel". We use all the games and mixers as "Immunity Challenges" and pass around a "Big D Idol" to each winning team. We keep track of all the winners and at the end of the weekend we declare the winning tribe and award them with a bag of candy to share. There are many ways you can incorporate the "Survivor" theme into the weekend to increase interest and participation. It adds excitement, teamwork and makes a great theme for the weekend.

TAKE IT TO THE CROSS

Incorporating a cross in your room to emphasize God's forgiveness and their need to forgive themselves and others can be very powerful. One way is to take their band aids they came up with during Hurts Band-Aids Can't Cover and place them at the foot of the cross. Or they can write people they need to forgive on an index card and place them at the foot of the cross. They can also consider ways in which God needs to forgive them and things they need to ask forgiveness for and place them at the foot of the cross. Having an actual cross in the room has a way of making it more personal and more real for the teens. This is another great opportunity to be playing some soft music in the background. (See Reflective Songs in the Attachment Section.)

THANK YOU CARDS

Bring in some extra note cards from home. Have each teen write a thank you note to the church for providing "The Big D". You can also include some of the Light Bulb Moments or the Chain of Hope to share with pastors, church leaders and others showing how life changing "The Big D" has been for these teens.

See attachment section

THREE MONTH GOALS

It is a good idea to encourage your teens to write some personal, spiritual, and family goals. To help them do this you can also hand out an envelope and ask them to self address it. After they fill out their three month goals (see attachment section), fold them and seal them in the envelope. At the end of the session collect them and tell them that in three months you will be mailing them as a reminder of the goals they set and to reflect on how they are doing.

THUMBALL

"The game that gets everybody talking."

This ball is a great idea to promote opening conversation and encourage teens in breaking the ice. It is a great mixer or ice breaker idea. Thumball™ transforms a ball, the toy everyone knows and loves, into a playful interactive game for education, training, entertainment, and promotion.

Throw it. Catch it. Look under a thumb. React to it!™

Thumballs are pleasingly squeezable with something printed on every panel. They add fun to any situation. There are 13 different balls with different activities to choose from. We have used the Ice Breaker, Who Are You, and Emotion Mania balls.

For more information or to order your thumball, please go to www.catch32ball.com.

See attachment section

TIMELINE OF CHANGES

It is important for the teens to realize that change happens to everyone throughout life, whether we like it or not. We are constantly having to adapt to new situations and new surroundings. As a way of demonstrating this point make copies of the Time Line in the Attachment Section and hand out a copy to each teen. First ask them to list on the bottom of the Time Line changes they have experienced due to their parents separation. Then ask them to look at their life and from the time they were been born to the time their parents separated and mark at least five changes, on the Time Line, that have happened and have had to adapt to. For instance, a grandparents death, a move, a different school, friends or family moving away etc.

Nugget of Truth – Discuss how many of changes they have had to adjust to since the separation and the amount of time they have had compared to their whole time line of changes. With a divorce many changes happen in a very short period of time thus making it even harder to handle and accept. Remind them to be patient with themselves and allow themselves the time needed to adapt. Encourage them that each change will come easier with time.

TRUE OR FALSE

See attachment section

Before group starts, make a True/False sign for everyone (see attachments). Hand out one sign per person. Ask the True/False questions found in the Attachments Section and have everyone hold up their sign as to whether they think it is True or False. Explain that this activity is not a test, it is an informal way of teaching truths of forgiveness. Make sure after each question you go into the explanation (see attachments) as to whether it was True or False and why.

TWISTER MIXER

See attachment section

This is a great mixer to encourage involvement by all the teens and to help them recognize that they are not alone in dealing with their parents separation or divorce.

1. You will need a Twister mat.
2. Depending on how many teens you have you may need to tape 2 or 4 twister mats together.
3. Read the situations found in the Attachments Section and have everyone who pertains to that situation follow what it says.
4. You may mix up the order for variety.
5. You may add any others that you choose.
6. Object of the game:
   > Have fun
   > Get teens to mix and mingle
   > Help them realize they are not the only ones in these situations
   > Help them discover what they have in common

Leaders Note: You may want to use separate mats for males and females.

VANNA

When doing The Wheel of Fortune (see Wheel of Fortune on page 34) it is always fun to have someone play "Vanna". It can be a teen or a volunteer leader. Either way it adds to the fun every time to see who "Vanna" will be. Remember, "Vanna" will need to be informed beforehand, of the puzzle answers that will be revealed. It is helpful, if you come prepared with the phrase written on an index card for "Vanna" to use. To add a little fun, bring a wig for "Vanna" to wear.

VIDEOS FOR TEENS

Two good videos for teens that are experiencing their parents divorce are listed below. They can be used at any time.

Dear Distant Dad – by Vision Video
This movie is especially good for any one who is dealing with an absent father. In this emotionally charged video, teenagers open their hearts with a rare and raw honesty to reveal the devastating hurt they feel inside when the relationships with their fathers change due to a separation and divorce. Teens will find that they are not alone and will better understand what some of their peers are going through. This DVD may be purchased at www.visonvideo.com, search under Dear Distant Dad or Product #501069D. The cost is $15.99.

When Mom and Dad Break Up – by Alan Thicke
This is a great movie for children to see that they are not alone in their feelings. This movie is focused more towards younger teens so consider the ages of your teens before selecting this video. You may purchase this video at www.amazon.com or www.imdb.com, search under When Mom and Dad Break Up. Prices vary.

WHEEL OF FORTUNE

See attachment section

This is a creative way of introducing the topics before each session. As you prepare you will need to print each letter (see attachments) and place them upside down in word order on the wall. When it is time to start have each teen take turns guessing a letter. If they guess a correct letter they get to take a guess at the entire phrase. If they either guess a wrong letter or did not guess the correct phrase it goes on to the next player. This continues until all the letters are revealed or the correct phrase is guessed.

To add a little twist, include a "Vanna" (see Vanna on page 33) with this activity.

Wheel of Fortune Rules

1. One person can only select one letter at a time. If their letter is correct they can take a guess at the phrase, but they cannot select another letter.
2. Vowels are no different than consonants.
3. Make sure everyone takes turns.
4. Comma's, apostrophes', dashes, etc. get revealed before the game begins.
5. They must guess the entire phrase, not one word at a time.
6. If there is more than one of the letter guessed, all of that same letters in the phrase must be revealed.

WHO AM I?

Hand out an index card to everyone as they enter the room. Tell them to write their first name vertically on the card, one letter at a time. After that, ask them to come up with a descriptive word or phrase about themselves that starts with that letter of the alphabet. When finished go around the room and have everyone share about themselves.

Give me an "A"

EXAMPLES:
B – Basketball player
E – Exhausted
T – Tall
H – Happy

Or

L - Lonely
A - Anxious
U - Unhappy
R – Rambunctious
A - Angry

WHO'S GOT THE CHARMIN?

At the beginning of a session pass around a roll of toilet paper and ask every teen to take some and pass it around. When the toilet paper roll has made it around tell everyone they need to share something for every section of TP they took.

Examples:
- Favorite memories
- Feelings over the last week
- Changes they've experienced
- Positive statements about the person on their left
- Something about themselves

YOUTUBE

There is an excellent You Tube video called "Baggage". It is approx. 5 ½ minutes in length but is very powerful. It is great to use as a way to present the need to your church, gain interest for your upcoming groups, or to play during a session. Go to www.youtube.com and search under "Baggage".

YOU'VE GOT MAIL

Have a mailbox available every week where they can leave anonymous questions they come up with throughout the weeks. You can either answer these questions weekly or you can accumulate them for a Panel Discussion. (See Panel Discussion on page 23)

Anger Thermometer

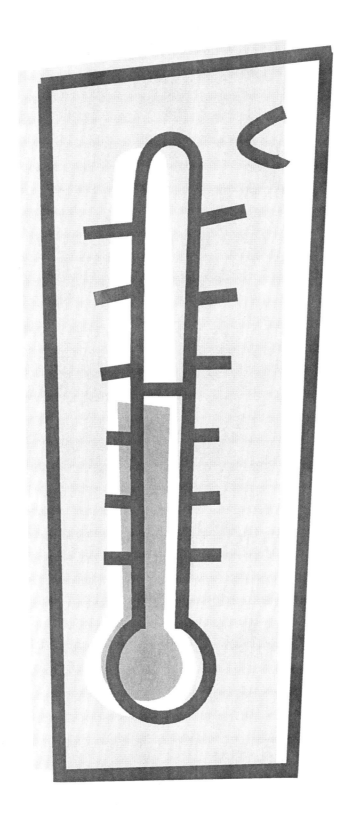

Sometimes I wish my family was more…..

I'm glad my family……..

Sometimes I wish my family would….

My family thinks I am….

One thing I wish I could change about my family is ….

One of the best things our family ever did together was…

My favorite family member who I do not live with is…. Why?

The family member I can talk to the easiest is…

I wish my parents would understand…

The saddest moment in my life was…

One of my favorite thing to do with my family is...

One of my favorite family memories is...

One of the things I miss most about my family being together is...

One of my favorite things to do with my mom is...

One of my favorite things to do with my dad is...

One thing I fear the most is...

One person whom I admire most is...
Why?

My true happiness comes from...

Sometimes I wish I was _____ years old.
Why?

I enjoy spending time....

One of the things I do best is...

My least favorite chore is ....

On of the best things about having two homes is...

On of the worst things about having two homes is...

One of the best things about being a teenager is...

One of the worst things about being a teenager is...

I am looking forward to.... Why?

Big D Quotes

Getting angry is easy, but keeping anger makes it hard to be happy. I was always angry & depressed but denying it.
                                                                                                      Janet—age 14

I had to see a counselor for a few months because I was depressed and suicidal. My anger wasn't controlled either; is always came out at the wrong times.
                                                                                                      Venessa—age 16

I felt lonely because dad never talked to me - only to my brothers and sister. Also, I'm the oldest, and I always did everything when my mom worked.
                                                                                                      Danny—age 16

The hardest stage for me to get through was depression. That was the stage I spent most of my life in. It took me a long time to get through this and begin to open up to people.
                                                                                                      Kate—age 15

Fear of rejection is the hardest feeling that plagues me. I don't want to get close to anyone for fear that they will reject me. I am learning, however, that my dad did not reject me; he rejected responsibility that was asked of him.
                                                                                                      Alan—age 17

I feel that it is very healthy to cry. Without it we would have a lot of built-up hurt. My parents have different points of view and different feelings about the divorce. Whenever I'm feeling hurt I usually wind up crying in the arms of my friends. After I have finished, the built-up repressed feelings have burst out.
                                                                                                      Teri– age 16

I think that it's okay to cry, depending on the situation. Sometimes I cry because I feel sad, but other times I find myself crying and feeling sorry for myself, thinking about me and not my heavenly Father. Instead of wasting my time and feeling sorry for myself I need to concentrate on all the good things God has taught me through my parents' divorce. The hurt of divorce will always be with me, but not at the same level it was when I first heard about it. As the years go by the hurt lessens, but it will always be there because it can't be taken from my memories. Something is said or done that triggers certain memories about my family, and I have to start over with my healing.
                                                                                                      Billy—age 16

I thought it was my fault because I was getting bad grades and getting in trouble a lot. Even when I was good my Dad would tell me to go outside or to go to my room for no reason at all.
                                                                                                      David– age 13

Yes, I thought it was my fault because sometimes I would ask if I could have a friend over, and my did would yell, saying no and then my mom would yell at him for yelling at me.
                                                                                                      Angelica—age 13

It feels like I'm the one that made them get divorced. It's hard on me because I am in the middle, and sometimes I feel that people don't care, but they do. Some days I feel like running away from everything, but I know that will not help me.
                                                                                                      Demichael– age 14

The wounds will eventually heal, but there will always be a deep scar to remind me of the pain I suffered.
                                                                                                      Shelly—age 15

I think that God is right there with me, crying when I cry, hurting when I hurt. He cares for me and has compassion.
                                                                                                      Thad—age 13

God is when I hurt, but then I realize that he is always there and I can talk to Him. Sometimes I kind of get mad because I do hurt. I cry a lot , but I guess that He is always there because He takes good care of us. When I'm hurting I always feel better when I talk to God.
                                                                                                      Ricky– age 14

How did I respond to the news that my parents were separated and getting divorced? I guess I went into shock. I thought my world was falling apart right in front of my face. I didn't know what to think. After I realized what was going on, I got real depressed and got sick a lot. I kept to myself because I didn't think anyone would understand, and I didn't take anyone's advice because I couldn't trust anymore.
                                                                                                      Mary—age 16

B	I	N	G	O
WHO HAS A STEP-SISTER	WHO GOES TO YOUR SAME CHURCH	WHOSE BOTH PARENTS HAVE REMARRIED	WHO LIVES IN A BLENDED FAMILY	WHO GOES TO YOUR SCHOOL
WHO IS AN ONLY CHILD	WHO HAS THE SAME NUMBER OF SIBLINGS AS YOU	WHO IS YOUNGER THAN YOU	WHO HAS A PARENT LIVING OUT OF STATE	WHO HAS BEEN TO THE BIG D BEFORE
WHOSE NAME STARTS WITH THE SAME LETTER AS YOUR NAME	WHO LIVES WITH THEIR STEP-DAD	FREE	WHO LIVES IN AN APARTMENT	WHO LIVES IN A DIFFERENT TOWN THAN YOU
WHO GOES TO A DIFFERENT SCHOOL	WHO HAD TO MOVE BECAUSE OF THEIR DIVORCE	WHO IS YOUR SAME AGE	WHO IS OLDER THAN YOU	WHO HAS A HALF BROTHER OR SISTER
WHO LIVES WITH THEIR STEP-MOM	WHOSE PARENTS ARE CURRENTLY SEPARATED AND NOT DIVORCED	WHO IS A STEP-BROTHER	WHO HAS 6 OR MORE GRAND PARENTS	WHO LIVES IN A SINGLE PARENT HOME

Blue Fish Video Clips

Session One - (Overview) Divorce Leaves Teen Divided Between Two Parents

Session Two - (The Grief Cycle) Finding Hope: Doug Fields
                                                          Struggling With Parents Divorce

Session Three - (Anger) Divorce Leads to Anger and Violence
                                        Angry at God: Doug Fields

Session Four - (Who's to Blame?) Out of Control: A Product of Divorce

Session Five - (Self-Esteem) Finding Your Identity: Chris Hill

Session Six - (Comfort) Bad Home Environment

Session Seven - (Feelings) Caught Between Divorced Parents

Session Eight - (Single Parent Homes) Rebuilding a Family After Divorce

Session Nine - (Blended Family Homes) Honoring Your Parents

Session Ten - (Forgiveness) Betrayed by Your Mother
                                          Forgiving Others: Doug Fields

Session Eleven - (Acceptance) Jennifer Knapp

Session Twelve - (Moving On) Looking to Sex for Love
                                          Filling the Empty Life

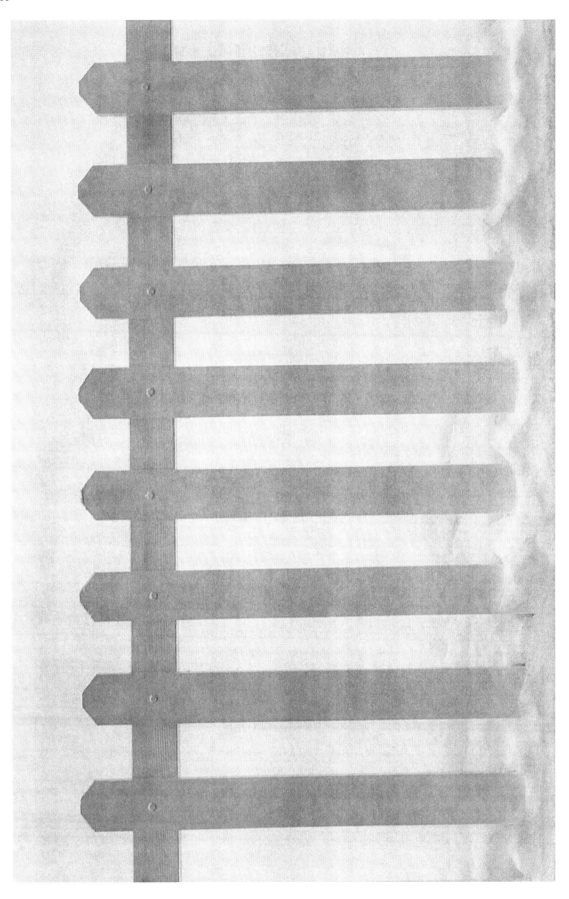

Chains of Hope

Cut strips of colored paper before the group begins. At the completion of this exercise you will end up with a colorful paper chain sharing ways they have changed for the better and what they have learned over the weeks through "The Big D".

Hand out strips of paper with markers and glue to every table. Ask everyone to write on the strips of paper things they have learned, changed, or benefited from since attending "The Big D". Leaders you can participate in this activity too. Once everyone has written 5 or 6 things, have them glue their strips into a circle, linking them all together. When everyone is finished making their own links, continue by linking everyone's together and make one long chain. Share with them how exciting it is to see how this chain of links is a true representation of the last few weeks together. We have come together because of a common experience and we have learned together, grown together, and developed lasting friendships. Our lives now represent a "Chain of Hope" for the world to see.

Examples of things they could put on their strips:

Grieving is normal and necessary

It is okay to cry

Forgiveness is not excusing the wrong

Nothing can separate me from God's love

I can love both parents equally

I don't have to be put in the middle

It was not my fault

I have a support system I can trust

I am made in the image of Christ

I am not the only one who feels this way

I can still have a promising future

I have a better relationship with my Mom/Dad now

There is more peace around the house

I'm more accepting of my step dad/mom

I'm more of a help around the house

I now have Jesus living in my heart

God does care about my hurts

My future is not doomed to divorce

Anger is not a sin

I've discovered my anger warning signs

I learned coping skills when I get angry

I do not have to be the messenger between my mom and dad

Hebrews 13:6a So we say with confidence, "The Lord is my helper; I will not be afraid. What can man do to me?"	**Psalm 145:13b,14,18** The Lord is faithful in all He says; He is gracious in all He does. The Lord helps the fallen and lifts up those bent beneath their loads. The Lord is close to all who call on Him, yes, to all who call on Him sincerely.
Psalm 139:2-5 You know everything I do; from far away You understand all my thoughts. You see me, whether I am working or resting; You know all my actions. Even before I speak, you already know what I will say. You are all around me on every side; You protect me with Your power.	**John 14:16-17a,18** {Jesus speaking} "I will ask the Father, and He will give you another Comforter, who will never leave you. He is the Holy Spirit, who leads in to all truth...I will not abandon you as orphans – I will come to you."
Psalms 46:1 God is our refuge and strength, an ever-present help in trouble.	**Psalm 102:17** God will listen to the prayers of the destitute. He will not reject their pleas. The Lord watches over those who fear Him, those who rely on His unfailing love.
Matt. 28:20b Surely I am with you always, to the very end of age.	**2 Corinthians 1:3-7** He comforts us in all our troubles so that we can comfort others. When others are troubled, we will be able to give them the same comfort God has given us. You can be sure that the more we suffer for Christ, the more God will shower us with His comfort through Christ.
Isaiah 66:13a As a mother comforts her child, so will I comfort you;	**Jeremiah 31:13b** I will turn their mourning into gladness; I will give them comfort and joy instead of sorrow.

Family Chair Game

Arrange a circle of chairs and have everyone sit on a chair. Read each statement one at a time and if the statement applies to them have them do what it says.

If you have an older sister, move one chair to the left.

If you have a dog in your home, move 3 chairs to the right.

If you have 2 grandfathers who are still living, move one chair to the left.

If your mom and dad are still living in the same home, move 2 chairs to the right.

If you have a younger brother, move 3 chairs to the left.

If you have 2 sisters, move 3 chairs to the right.

If you have a step mom, move 2 chairs to the left.

If you have a grandmother who lives in a different state other than Minnesota, move 1 chair to the right.

If your mom and dad are separated and not divorced, move one chair to the left.

If you have a step brother or sister, move 2 chairs to the left.

If your mom and dad live in 2 separate towns ,move 3 chairs to the right.

If you have a half brother or sister, move 2 chairs to the right.

If you have 3 or more siblings (half, whole or step), move 3 chairs to the left.

If one parent is still single and one has remarried, move 2 chairs to the right.

If you have a step dad, move 1 chair to the right.

If you have a grand parent living with you, move 3 chairs to the left.

Family Change Game

Bring in enough M&M's, Skittles or, Jelly Beans for the amount of teens you have attending.
Pass out the candy and read the statements below.

FAMILY CHANGE STATEMENTS

If your parents are divorced, take one.
If you had to move into a different home, take two.
If you have a step parent, take one.
If you are still living in the same home prior to the separation, take one.
If you talk disrespectful to either of your parents, put back two.
If you had to change schools, take three.
If you now have a step sibling, take one.
If you had to give away your pet, take three.
If you find yourself purposely trying to stay away from home, put back three.
If you now have to share your room, take two.
If you had to make new friends, take one.
If you've lied in the past 24 hours, put back one.
If you live with your dad, take one.
If you got angry yesterday, put back two.
If your mom had to get a job, take two.
If your parents are only separated and not divorced, take one.
If you see a counselor or school counselor, take two.
If one of your parents has a girlfriend/boyfriend, take two.
If you argue with your parents a lot put, back two.
If your mom changed her last name, take one.
If you have to do more chores now, take one.
If you have skipped school, put back three
If one of your parents has remarried, take two.
If you had to get a job, take one.
If you argue with your sister or brother, put back two.
If you had to move to a different town, take two.
If one of your parents lives out of state, take three.
If you live with your mom, take one.
If you live with another family member (Grandpa & Grandma), take three.
If you were an only child now you have step siblings, take three.
If both your parents are remarried, take two.

Feelings Activity Box

Collect as many of the following items as possible and put them into a box. Keep the box in a convenient place so you can use it whenever you are having trouble expressing your feelings. Choose an item or two that will help you get your feelings out in a healthy way.

Pillow: Hit it when you are angry. Cry into it when you are sad. Squeeze it when you need a hug.

Telephone: Call someone you trust and talk about your feelings. Call a friend, a pastor, or a trusted relative.

Notebook and Pen: Journal your feelings. Write a poem. Draw a picture.

Stationery and Envelopes: Write a letter about your feelings and give it to someone you trust. Remember, you don't have to send every letter. Sometimes you just need to get things out on paper.

Drawing Supplies: Drawing or scribbling helps get your feelings out.

Box of Kleenex: For every time you just need to cry!!

Feeling Activity Box

 Running Shoes: Doing something physical helps get your feelings out.

 Stuffed Animal: Hold it when you feel alone. Squeeze it when you need a hug. Talk to it when you need to talk.

 Computer: E-mail a trusted friend or a caring relative. Journal your thoughts.

 Large Red Heart: Talk to someone you love about your feelings. Ask for a hug.

Feelings Box Activity

Prepare a Feelings Box from the previous page. Go through the box one item at a time and as you hand out each item explain how they could be used to help you get your feelings out. When you have emptied the box and everyone has an item from the box read the following scenarios and ask how they could use the items they are holding to deal with the situations in a healthy way.

Scenarios

* Your parents have just told you they are getting a divorce.

* Your dad promises to take you somewhere special and then cancels at the last minute.

* Your mom introduces you to her new boyfriend.

* It's your dad's weekend to have you and he doesn't show up.

* Your step mom says something mean to you.

* You overhear your mom and dad fighting about you.

* Your dad drills you about your mom's life and who she is seeing.

* You want a new outfit or new pair of shoes and your mom says she can't afford it anymore.

* Your mom says you can go to the movies but your step dad says no so now you have to stay home.

* Your mom asks you to ask your dad for the child support money or to pay for half a doctors bill.

* Your dad calls to invite you to Valley Fair this weekend and your mom says no because you are with her this weekend.

* You come home from school and you see your mom crying on the couch.

* You have a parents night for a school event and your parents refuse to sit together.

* You invite both of your parents to your concert and your mom tells you she refuses to go if your dad comes.

* You go to your dads and within an hour of being there he leaves you to go out on a date.

* Your mom is dating someone you really don't like and is always expecting you to stay home and babysit.

* Your mom has left and abandoned the family.

* Your mom is never home anymore because she has had to get a job.

* You bring your friends home and your mom has been drinking.

* You want to spend more time at your dad's place but your mom won't let you.

53

Feelings Alphabet Race

A B C D E F G H I J K L M

N O P Q R S T U V W X Y Z

Feelings Words

Abandoned	Betrayed	Crabby	Dreadful	Helpless
Accepted	Bitter	Cranky	Eager	Hesitant
Accused	Bored	Crappy	Ecstatic	High
Aching	Bothered	Crazy	Edgy	Hollow
Adventurous	Boxed-in	Critical	Elated	Hopeful
Affectionate	Brave	Criticized	Embarrassed	Horrified
Aggravated	Breathless	Crushed	Empty	Hostile
Aggressive	Bristling	Cuddly	Enraged	Humiliated
Agony	Broken-up	Curious	Enraptured	Hung Up
Agreeable	Bruised	Cut	Enthusiastic	Hurt
Alienated	Bubbly	Damned	Enticed	Hyper
Alive	Bugged	Daring	Esteemed	Ignorant
Alone	Burdened	Deceived	Exasperated	Impatient
Aloof	Burned	Deceptive	Exhilarated	Impressed
Alluring	Callous	Degraded	Exposed	Incompetent
Amazed	Calm	Delighted	Fascinated	Incomplete
Amused	Capable	Demeaned	Flattered	Independent
Angry	Captivated	Demoralized	Foolish	Innocent
Anguished	Carefree	Dependent	Forced	Insecure
Annoyed	Careful	Depressed	Forceful	Insignificant
Anxious	Careless	Deprived	Fortunate	Insincere
Apart	Caring	Deserted	Forward	Inspired
Apologetic	Carried Away	Desirable	Friendly	Insulted
Appreciative	Cautious	Desirous	Frightened	Intimate
Apprehensive	Certain	Despair	Frustrated	Intolerant
Approved	Chased	Desperate	Full	Involved
Argumentative	Cheated	Destroyed	Funny	Irate
Aroused	Cheerful	Different	Furious	Irked
Astonished	Choked Up	Dirty	Generous	Irresponsible
Assertive	Close	Disappointed	Genuine	Irritated
Attached	Cold	Disconnected	Giddy	Jealous
Attacked	Comfortable	Disgraced	Giving	Jittery
Attentive	Comforted	Disgruntled	Grateful	Joyous
Attractive	Competitive	Disgusted	Greedy	Left Out
Aware	Complacent	Distant	Grim	Lively
Awestruck	Complete	Distraught	Grouchy	Lonely
Badgered	Confident	Distressed	Grumpy	Loose
Baited	Conflicted	Distrusted	Guarded	Lost
Battered	Confused	Distrustful	Happy-go-lucky	Loving
Beaten	Considerate	Dominated	Hard	Loved
Beautiful	Consumed	Domineering	Hassled	Low
Belittled	Content	Doomed	Hateful	Lucky
Belligerent	Cool	Double-crossed	Healthy	Lustful
Bereaved	Coy	Down	Helpful	Mad

Feelings Words

Malicious
Mean
Miserable
Misunderstood
Moody
Mystified
Nasty
Nervous
Numb
Obsessed
Offended
Open
Ornery
Out of Control
Overwhelmed
Overjoyed
Pampered
Panicky
Paralyzed
Patient
Peaceful
Peeved
Perceptive
Perturbed
Petrified
Phony
Pleased
Powerless
Pressured
Proud
Pulled Apart
Put-Down
Puzzled
Quarrelsome
Quiet
Ravished
Ravishing
Real
Refreshed
Regretful
Rejected
Rejecting
Relaxed
Relieved

Removed
Repulsed
Repulsive
Resentful
Resistant
Responsible
Responsive
Revengeful
Rotten
Ruined
Safe
Satiated
Satisfied
Scared
Scolded
Scorned
Screwed
Secure
Seduced
Seductive
Self-centered
Self-conscious
Selfish
Separated
Shattered
Shocked
Shot-down
Shy
Sickened
Silly
Sincere
Sinking
Smart
Smothered
Smug
Sneaky
Snowed
Soft
Soothed
Sorry
Spiteful
Spontaneous
Squelched
Starved

Stiff
Stifled
Stimulated
Strangled
Strong
Stubborn
Stunned
Stupid
Subdued
Submissive
Successful
Suffocated
Sure
Sweet
Sympathetic
Tainted
Tender
Tense
Terrific
Terrified
Thrilled
Ticked
Tickled
Tight
Timid
Tired
Tolerant
Tormented
Torn
Tortured
Trapped
Tremendous
Tricked
Trustful
Ugly
Unapproachable
Unaware
Uncertain
Uncomfortable
Under Control
Understanding
Understood
Unfriendly
Unhappy

Unimportant
Unimpressed
Unstable
Upset
Uptight
Useful
Valuable
Valued
Violated
Violent
Vulnerable
Warm
Weak
Whipped
Whole
Wild
Willing
Wiped-out
Withdrawn
Wishful
Wonderful
Worried
Worthy
Wounded
Zapped

"Get Off My Back"

FEELINGS

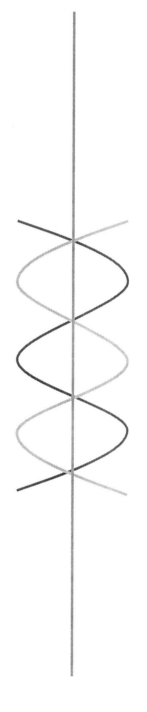

GUILT

ANGER

BLAME

FRUSTRATION

JEALOUSY

HURT

FEAR

NUMB

WORRY

UGLY

QUIET

ANXIOUS

SELFISH

RELIEVED

ANNOYED

SILLY

SURPRISED

DISCOURAGED

INSECURE

CALM

HELPLESS

MISERABLE

HOPEFUL

FUNNY

IMPATIENT

MISUNDERSTOOD

EXCITED

NERVOUS

PHONY

NEUTRAL

TERRIBLE

NEEDY

LOVED

STRESSED

TIRED

SAD

DEPRESSED

MAD

REJECTED

EMPTY

ALONE

SCARED

SORRY

NEGLECTED

UNHAPPY

ASHAMED

BITTER

UNAPPRECIATED

UPSET

CONFUSED

BRAVE

EXHAUSTED

HAPPY

LONELY

OVERWHELMED

IRRITATED

PESSIMISTIC

GRATEFUL

INDIFFERENT

RESENTFUL

JUDGED

GLAD

LOYAL

OPTIMISTIC

STRONG

SECURE

Hurts Band-Aids Can't Cover

Here are some examples to get things rolling.

⇒ Loss of both parents in the same home

⇒ Feeling rejected by either parent

⇒ Loss of friends

⇒ Loss of home

⇒ Hearing parents fighting

⇒ Feeling like being torn between 2 homes

⇒ Seeing mom or dad hurting

⇒ Feeling abandoned by a parent

⇒ Loss of grandparents

⇒ Feeling it was their fault (that they did something wrong)

⇒ Blame

⇒ Loneliness

⇒ Questioning why God isn't answering their prayers

⇒ Feeling stuck in the middle

⇒ Mixed loyalties

⇒ Having to move

⇒ Missing your parent not living with you

⇒ Jealous of boyfriend/girlfriend/new spouse or step children who get to live with other parent

⇒ Loss of dreams

⇒ Loss of planned family vacations

⇒ Hurts from overhearing things said between parents in arguments

⇒ Loss of a pet

⇒ Questioning God' love for you

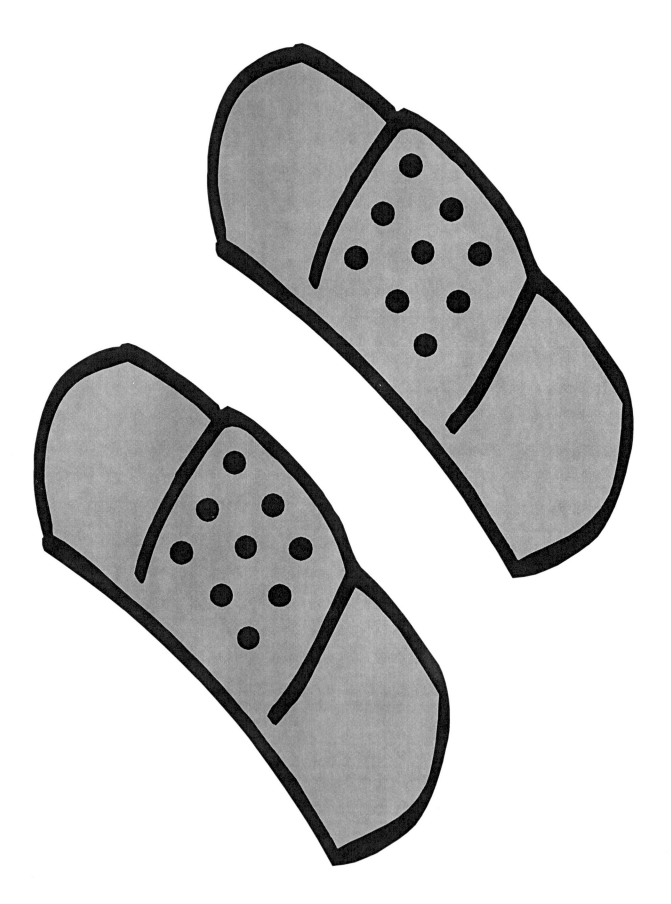

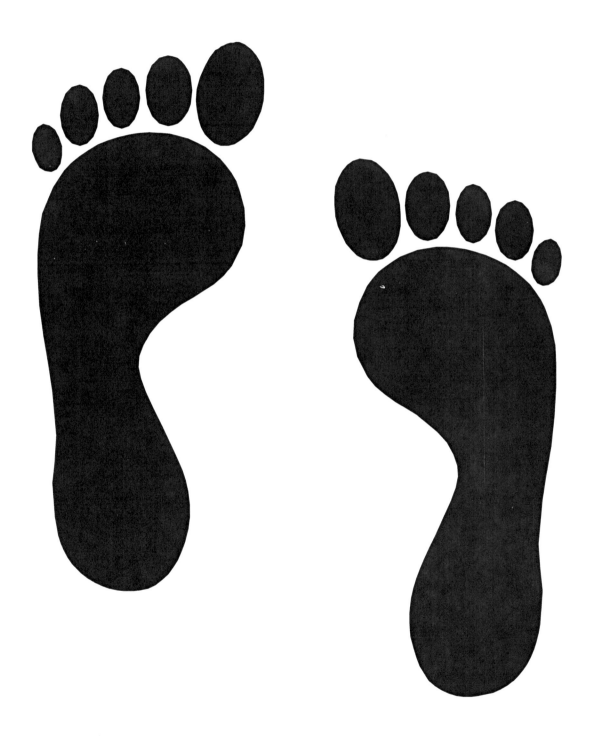

"IN THEIR SHOES"

Julie shares a room with her little sister, Jessica. Her stepsister, Monica, has her own room

After school one day, Julie goes into Monica's room and starts listening to one of her CD's. Monica walks in.

How might Monica feel?

How might Julie feel?

"IN THEIR SHOES"

Rachel is waiting for her Dad to pick her up from school, so they can go for their Friday "pizza and movie night". Instead Rachel's step-mom comes to pick her up and tells her that her Dad won't be able to go, but she'll be happy to take Rachel. Rachel barely says a word to her step-mom all evening.

How is Rachel feeling?

How might her step-mom be feeling?

"IN THEIR SHOES"

Ben is fishing with his step-dad.
He has been fishing all day with no luck.
Suddenly he catches a big fish. He is so excited!
"I can't wait to tell Dad!" He says.
He shows his step-dad, but his step-dad has no reaction.

What might Ben be feeling?

How about his step-dad?

"IN THEIR SHOES"

Josh comes home from his Dad's and can't wait to hook up his new video game he got for Christmas. His younger step-brother, Eric, comes in and tells him he wants to try it out too.

How might Josh feel?

How might Eric feel?

"IN THEIR SHOES"

Andy has an X-box. His step-brother, Billy, doesn't have one at his Mom's or Dad's homes.

When Andy gets home from school, he really wants to kick back and play a game. But Billy has some friends over and they are playing a game.

How would Andy handle this situation?

What could Billy be feeling?

"IN THEIR SHOES"

Brittany is in the middle of watching a TV show when her step-brother Eric walks in to watch his favorite show.

Brittany's step-dad, Eric's dad, picks up the remoteand changes the channel.

How might Brittany feel?

How about Eric? The step-dad?

"IN THEIR SHOES"

Mark's mom is dropping him off at his dad's house for a visit when he overhears his dad telling his Mom that he will not be able to have him visit during Christmas break this year.

Mark's dad will be going out of town with his wife and stepchildren for the holidays.

How might Mark feel?

How might his dad feel?

"IN THEIR SHOES"

Dan watched an "R" rated movie at his mom's. When he gets back home, he tells his older brother, Steve, what a cool movie it was.

Steve then asks to watch it. Steve's mom said "no" right away because of it's rating.

What is Steve feeling?

Steve's mom?

"IN THEIR SHOES"

Susan wants to go to a movie tonight. Her step-dad says "no" and wants to wait until next weekend when his kids are with him. You have checked and the movie you wanted to see will not be there next week.

How would this make Susan feel?

How might her step-dad be feeling?

"IN THEIR SHOES"

Joe is in the middle of playing a video game when his step-dad asks him to take out the trash.

He tells his step-dad that he'll do it in a minute. Thirty minutes later, the trash is still there, and Joe's step-dad asks him again to take out the trash.

This time, frustration comes out of his voice.

How might Joe feel?

What about his step-dad?

"IN THEIR SHOES"

Sarah hurries to set the table for dinner before her step-mom comes home from work.

In her rush, she drops the vase of flowers on the floor, and the step-mom's vase breaks.

How might Sarah feel?

"IN THEIR SHOES"

When Carrie comes home from her dad's, she finds out her mom and step-family all went camping while she was gone. That is all they talked about at supper.

How would Carrie feel?

How about Carrie's mom?

"IN THEIR SHOES"

Jon is 17 and has his driver's license. When he comes to his mom's house, he always has to drive his younger step-sister, Suzie, everywhere. Jon gets tired of being the errand boy.

How would Jon feel week after week?

What about Suzie?

"IN THEIR SHOES"

"IN THEIR SHOES"

Jenny goes to her Dad's house every other weekend. Whenever Jenny is at her dad's she has to baby-sit her 4 year old step-sister, Cathy, while Dad takes his new wife out for dinner.

Jenny gets frustrated and says, "Why is it always my responsibility to watch the "little brat" again?

What is Jenny feeling?

How does this make Cathy feel?

"IN THEIR SHOES"

Dear God,   .

_____

_____

_____

_____

_____

_____

_____

_____

_____

_____

_____

_____

_____

_____

_____

LETTER TO MOM

LETTER TO DAD

You may not see it at first, but the white spaces create the word OPTICAL, while the shadowed landscape spells out ILLUSION.

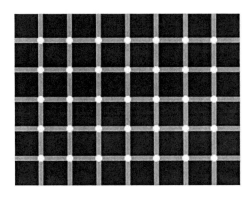

Can you count the black dots?

Are the horizontal lines parallel, or do they slope?

Optical Illusions

How many legs does this elephant have?

A rabbit, looking right? Or a duck, looking left?

Man playing a horn? Or woman's face?

Princess or a old woman?

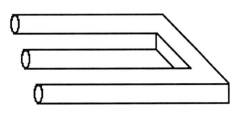

Three prong fork?

Optical Illusions

Stare at the dark dot in the center for 10 seconds...

Now move your head forward and backward.
As your head moves closer to your page
and then back away from your page, the circles
will appear to be spinning.
- But are they really spinning? Absolutely NOT! - - -

Rabbit or a Duck?

THINGS THAT MAKE ME HAPPY

.

THINGS THAT I WORRY ABOUT

THINGS THAT MAKE ME ANGRY

THING'S THAT MAKE ME SAD

THINGS THAT I WISH I COULD CHANGE

Pick Two

Possible items to put out for teens to pick from. Have each teen pick one item that represents who they were before their parents separated and one item that represents them after the divorce. When finished, go around the room and share why they picked these items.

An old tennis shoe	Lunch box
A bat	Candy
A cookie	Notebook
Dish soap	Battery
Toothbrush	Toy
Camera	Lego
CD	Deck of cards
Photo album	Earphones
Piece of gum	Coupon
Watch	A button
Glue	Eraser
Keys	Marker
Lotion	Remote control
Stapler	A ball
Credit card	Doll
Picture	A box
Ring	Movie
Pen	Dollar bill
Spoon	A coin
Glove	Refrigerator magnet
Cell phone	Kleenex
Hat	Paper Cup
Dryer sheet	Scissors

Pluses & Minuses

It is good to realize that all the changes we were resisting actually don't always have to turn out bad. Take some time and list some pluses and minuses that you have experienced because of your parents divorce.

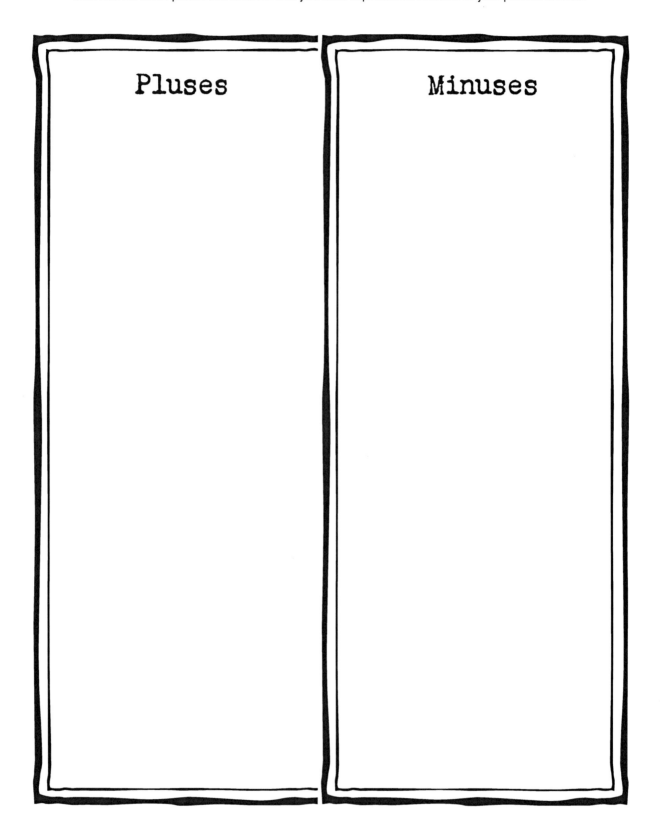

Pluses

Minuses

Philippians 4: 6 & 7

Do not be anxious about anything, but in everything, by prayer and petition with thanksgiving, present your requests to God. And the peace of God which transcends all understanding will guard your hearts and minds in Christ Jesus. (NIV)

Scripture Search Game

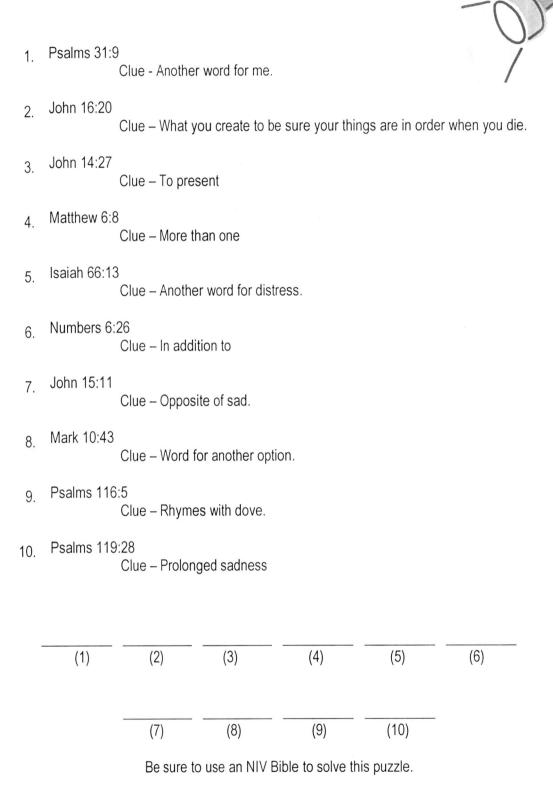

1. Psalms 31:9
   Clue - Another word for me.

2. John 16:20
   Clue – What you create to be sure your things are in order when you die.

3. John 14:27
   Clue – To present

4. Matthew 6:8
   Clue – More than one

5. Isaiah 66:13
   Clue – Another word for distress.

6. Numbers 6:26
   Clue – In addition to

7. John 15:11
   Clue – Opposite of sad.

8. Mark 10:43
   Clue – Word for another option.

9. Psalms 116:5
   Clue – Rhymes with dove.

10. Psalms 119:28
    Clue – Prolonged sadness

_____ _____ _____ _____ _____ _____
   (1)   (2)   (3)   (4)   (5)   (6)

_____ _____ _____ _____
   (7)   (8)   (9)   (10)

Be sure to use an NIV Bible to solve this puzzle.

Scripture Search Game Answers

1. Psalms 31:9
   Clue - Another word for me.

2. John 16:20
   Clue – What you create to be sure your things are in order when you die.

3. John 14:27
   Clue – To present

4. Matthew 6:8
   Clue – More than one

5. Isaiah 66:13
   Clue – Another word for distress.

6. Numbers 6:26
   Clue – In addition to

7. John 15:11
   Clue – Opposite of sad.

8. Mark 10:43
   Clue – Word for another option.

9. Psalms 116:5
   Clue – Rhymes with dove.

10. Psalms 119:28
    Clue – Prolonged sadness

I	will	give	them	comfort	and
(1)	(2)	(3)	(4)	(5)	(6)

	joy	instead	of	sorrow.	
	(7)	(8)	(9)	(10)	

Skits

Skit 1: The Fights

Brandon: "Hey Dad, can I have some money to go paint balling this Saturday with my friends?"

Dad: "Sure, a boy needs to have a good time while he can."

Mom (upon hearing the conversation): "Jim, what are you doing? You know that we don't' have the money right now to do needless things. I am sorry Brandon, but despite your father's lack of judgment if you want to do something with your friends you need to find your own money."

(mom and dad continue fighting in the background)

Brandon" (monologue) "Just a few months later my parents sat me and my brother down to tell us that they were getting a divorce. My heart broke. I just kept remembering all the fights they got into, me being the cause of most of them. What if I had just kept my mouth shut? What if I got a job so I didn't need to ask for money all the time? Maybe things would have been different."

Skit 2: The Surprise

Sharron: (monologue) "It was a special occasion. Mom and I would be hanging out all weekend. I thought it would be the best time in my life until that talk came along. I wasn't prepared for what she was about to tell me."

(turns to her mom on the bed beside her)

Mom: "Honey, I made this special trip for the two of us in hopes that we could talk. There is something really important I need to tell you. Dad is moving out this weekend while we are gone. He is moving in with another woman."

(mom freezes)

Sharron: (monologue) "I heard my heart hit the floor. There must be something wrong I thought. I must be imagining things. My Parents!! Not my parents!! Everyone else's parents get divorced but not mine. There were the perfect couple, everyone thought so. And the very idea of my dad living with another woman, who could even think such a thing? It must be a dream, a very horrible dream.

Skit 3: Between Lives

Dad: "So how is our mom doing these days?"

Megan: "Fine."

Dad: "Is she happy with Brad?"

Megan: "I think so."

Dad: "Well if she was wondering, I have a new girlfriend named Bobbi."

Megan: "Whatever Dad."

THE OTHER HOME

Mom: "How was your time at your dads?"

Megan: "Fine, I met his new girlfriend."

Mom: "What is she like? Probably not as nice as Brad."

Megan: "I wish you guys would just leave me out of it!"

Skit 4: Basketball

Jon: "Hey Dad, can I go out for basketball?"

Dad: "Of course you can."

Jon: "I need $140.00 to play on the team."

Dad: "That is your mother's responsibility. You know she has all the money, especially with all the child support I pay her. Ask her for it!"

THE OTHER HOME

Jon: "Mom, do you think I can have $140.00 to join the basketball team at school. Dad said it was okay I just had to ask you for the money."

Mom: "Your dad told you to ask me! I don't have the money to pay for that. I am busy paying for your clothes and all that food you eat. If he wants you to play basketball, he can pay for it!"

Skits

Scenario #1

"Hey, what's up? Is your dad coming to graduation?"

"He can't", I say. He'll be in Europe for a conference. It's not a big deal, though." I look away. There's no way I'm going to tell my friend that my parents have separated.

"Not a big deal? You're graduating with highest honors! I'd be so upset if my dad couldn't be there."

Yeah, but my dad will probably bring me lots of gifts just to make up for it." I force a smile.

My friend nods, but says nothing.

He will be there some day, says a voice inside my head, even though a part of me doesn't believe it. I wish I could tell my friend the real truth: My dad moved out for good, and I don't know when I'll hear from him again.

Some days I wonder if he will ever be involved in my life again. But then I remember how he used to talk with me and how he let me work in his office, and I know there's no way he will stay away for good. Besides, I have to have hope.

"At least you don't have to worry about him embarrassing you," my friend says with a frown. "My dad always takes so many stupid pictures."

I nod as if I understand, but inside I wonder if my dad has a picture of me anywhere. "I've got to see what Mr. Moser wants," I say quickly changing the subject. "It's about our next student counsel meeting," I throw in before heading to the principal's office. I check the empty student council mailbox and start talking with Mr. Moser's secretary, just in case anyone's watching.

Scenario #2

Lisa hears something tap the window. She gets up from the piano and looks outside, but everything looks the same. She stands there with her arms folded watching the cars zoom past on the busy street in front of her house. Everyone seems to know where they're going, but not her.

She still doesn't know why her parents had to get a divorce. Couldn't they have worked out their problems if they had gone to counseling? Did they really try hard enough?

She sits back down at the piano and turns to Chopin's Prelude in D-flat Major. She positions her fingers above the keys and plays the tranquil melody. She remembers the last conversation she heard between her parents. They were fighting about her grades. Her dad said they weren't good enough. Then he went on to blame her mother because she let Lisa spend so much time talking on the phone and hanging out that the mall. He also said Lisa should be doing more chores, especially cleaning her messy room.

Maybe if she had worked harder and been the type of daughter her dad had wanted, none of her parents' problems would have started.

Skits

The melody changes. It can't be ALL her fault. Her parents had been fighting for years. They must have fought about other things besides her.

She moves her right thumb up to hit the black G-sharp key over and over. Maybe she should have told her dad she loved him more often. Maybe that would have given him a reason to stay.

She plays the original melody again. She should have done more to try to fix things.

The melody softens. She wishes she knew more about why they had to get a divorce, so she wouldn't feel so confused all the time.

She stops playing, even though she hasn't finished the piece. She pulls the cover over the keyboard and turns off the piano light.

Scenario #3

Steve plants both his elbows on the TV tray and clutches his hands into a fist. He looks down every few minutes from the football game to his sheets of statistics. His sister, Mary, pokes her head in.

"Can you get me a cup of coffee?" he asks, then looks back at the TV.

Yeah, sure," Mary frowns, then leaves.

Steve knows there must be something she wants to talk about. The last thing his sister like s to do is watch sports.

Mary returns with a cup of coffee and sets it on the end table, away from his papers.

"The Vikings just scored another touchdown," he says. "There's no way the Packers will catch up now."

"They play so many games. What's it matter if they lose?"

Steve raised his eyebrows at her. "Don't you have something to do?" he asks, half joking, half serious.

"You're something," Mary throws in before leaving.

The Vikings win. Steve jumps up, clapping and yelling.

Mary comes back, shaking her head.

"Now, that's what I call a good victory," Steve says, tossing his pen on the TV tray.

"Any other games on?" Mary sits down in the recliner chair.

Steve continues paging through his statistics. "Not till tomorrow night."

Skits

"Steve, there's something I want to ask you."

"Yeah, go ahead." He jots down another figure.

Mary takes a deep breath and clasps her hands. "Looks like Mom wants us to meet her new boyfriend."

Steve shrugs his shoulders. *So what?* he thinks. *Mom doesn't really care about me. Why should I bother meeting her boyfriend?"*

Mary sits up. "She's invited us to dinner with them. I think we should go."

Steve glares at her. "I have better things to do."

"You know, Mom sounds a lot happier now. Maybe she'll start doing more things with us. I know it'll be different with this guy in the picture, but maybe we can be more like a family."

Steve grabs hold of the arms of his chair. "We don't have a family anymore, and we never will." He looks back at the TV and cracks his knuckles.

"I can't believe you're saying that!"

Steve continues to look away from her. He wishes he could have a normal family like his friends.

"Look, I know Mom hasn't treated you right, but maybe things will be better now."

Steve turns toward Mary. "Would you just get on with your life," he says slowly and calmly. He stares at her until she looks away. Then he looks back at the TV. All he can think about is how much his family isn't a family anymore. And now he and Mary will probably be replaced for good.

After a few minutes he asks, "What, is she planning to marry him or something?"

"I don't know. Probably. At least she cares enough to have us meet him."

"I don't know why you always get your hopes up. You'll only get disappointed again."

"It could be a lot worse, you know. She could have moved away and never seen us again."

Steve switches the channels. He knows that's true, but it still didn't make them a family.

"The dinner reservations are for 8:00 Friday at Michael's. That's this coming Friday."

"At least she picked a decent place to eat."

"You need to give people a second chance, Steve. It'll make your life a lot better."

"I love Mom, but I don't like her right now. Her boyfriend isn't going to change that. Nothing will. Can't you get that through your head?"

Mary storms out the room and slams the door.

Skits

Scenario #4

John turns away from the door and cups his hand over the phone. "I'd like to stay another week or so, Mom."

"Another week? You've already been there two weeks. That's a lot longer than we agreed on." She goes on to list all the projects she needs him to do at home: mow the lawn, clean the basement, sort through his old clothes for Goodwill to pick up.

"I know," John says, "but I'm really having fun. Dad has a boat, and he's teaching me how to water ski." He wants to mention that he's getting to know his dad better, but instead adds, "I'm getting pretty good."

"Is he still living with Roxanne, or has he found another bimbo? She's young enough to be your sister, you know."

John shakes his head. *Here it comes again*, he thinks. He agrees that it's wrong for his dad to be living with a woman he's not married to, but why should John be punished because of it? "She's not a bad person, Mom" he finally says.

"So he *is* still living with her. That man should rot…….."

Said the wrong thing again, John thinks. *Won't I ever learn to keep my mouth shut?*

"You know, Julie hasn't been able to get her grades because your father still hasn't paid the tuition bill. I bet he's spending a good bit on that tramp, though."

John remembers his father's advice: If your mother gives you any flack, tell her to get a life; you're old enough to make your own decisions. "I should be able to stay longer if I want to," John says.

"Go ahead and continue to treat him like a king, after all he's done to us."

"John," his father calls, "dinner's ready."

"Mom, I've got to go. I'll call you tomorrow."

A click sounds on the other end, then a dial tone.

John hangs up the phone, feeling like the most selfish person in the world….and the most confused.

Skit Scenes:

1. Your mom just told you that your family is going to move to New York. You don't want to go! You react by telling her you hate her and then you push your little brother out of the way as you storm out of the room.

2. You are trying to do your homework, but your parents are having another fight about their divorce. You feel too upset to concentrate. You put on your running shoes and go outside to run around the block a few times. When you come back you feel calmer and can concentrate again.

3. Your mom is getting remarried to a man you really like. But you are not sure how you are going to like sharing your mom with the new stepbrothers who are coming to live with you. You are spending a lot of time in your room, thinking about it. When your mom comes in and asks, "What's wrong?" You say, "Nothing. I just want to be left alone."

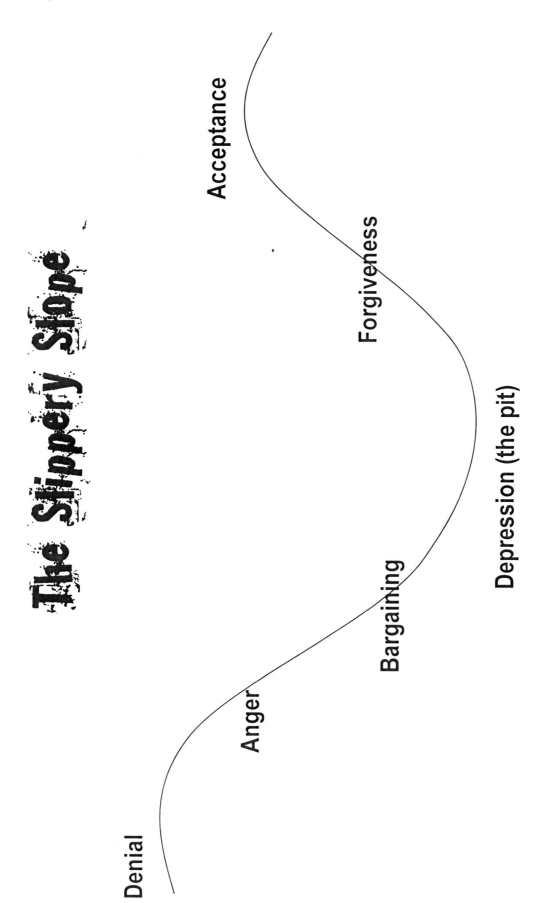

The Slippery Slope

Denial

Anger

Bargaining

Depression (the pit)

Forgiveness

Acceptance

Put an X on the slope where you think you are.

Solar System

Write your name in the sun, then inside each planet write the names of people in your support system. As you think of these people ask yourself these questions;

- who really listens to me
- who makes time for me
- who can I depend on
- is there someone who can be honest with me even when I don't want to hear it
- who has asked me how I am doing, who is always there for me
- if you were in trouble who would you call for help

DENIAL STAGE STATEMENTS

"Hey look I'm okay. It doesn't bother me."

"It's probably best for all of us."

"It's no big deal, they'll get back together."

"This isn't happening to me."

"He will be there for me someday."

ANGER STAGE STATEMENTS

"It's all your fault – Why are you doing this to me?"

"You ruined everything – I thought you loved me."

"Why don't you stop being so selfish, all you think about is yourself."

"I don't want to live with you anymore, I'm moving in with dad."

"What are my friends going to think – I don't want to be a part of this family anymore."

"What about me – What am I suppose to do?"

BARGAINING STAGE STATEMENTS

"Hey Mom, Dad was asking about you. I think he is still interested. You should give him a call."

"Dear God, if you get my parents back together, I'll never ask for another thing."

"Hey Dad, if you come pick me up maybe mom will be there and you can talk to her."

"I'll promise I'll be a better person if you and Dad get back together."

"Once I make the A Squad, Dad will make more time for me."

DEPRESSION STAGE STATEMENTS

"What good is life, anyway. Nothing is fun anymore."

"If it can't be the way it was then I don't want to be part of it"

"Go away. Leave me alone. Life stinks."

"If they don't want me, nobody will."

"I just don't care about anything anymore"

ACCEPTANCE STAGE STATEMENTS

"I don't like what has happened to my family but I'll be okay."

"I miss not having my mom and dad together but I have gotten to know my dad better now."

"This isn't the life I wanted but good can still come out of it."

"I know my mom and dad both love me but they just can't live together anymore."

"There is nothing I could have or have not done to cause my parents to divorce. It was their decision based on their choices."

"I cannot control what my mom or dad do, but I can control what I do."

Three Month Goals

1.

2.

3.

TIMELINE OF CHANGES

Parents
Separated

Changes since the separation:

1.

2.

3.

4.

5.

Birth

True or False Questions

Girls have more feelings than guys.

> False – we all have feelings. Girls usually just have an easier time showing them.

Big boys don't cry.

> False – There is no such thing as boys not crying. God made all of us with emotions and it is okay for everyone to show them and cry.

Everyone has the same feelings.

> False – God has made each one of us different. Although everyone has feelings they are all different.

Feelings like happy, excited, proud and love are okay to feel.

> True – These feelings as well as other feelings are great to feel, but feelings are not just limited to positive ones.

Feelings like sad, angry, hate and jealousy are NOT okay to feel.

> False – Although these feelings are more difficult, they are still okay to feel. It is very normal to feel these kinds of feelings while you are going through a separation or divorce in your family. It is not wrong to feel these feelings, it is usually how you choose to express them that makes them wrong.

Everyone expresses their feelings in the same way.

> False – God has made us all different and you will express your feelings depending on your unique personality.

It's okay to have feelings, but you should never let anyone know what they truly are.

> False – Most of your healing will come as you open up and share your feelings with someone you trust. The more you hold them in, the longer it will take to heal.

Only "scaredy cats" and "sissies" are afraid.

> False – When your parents are going through a separation or divorce it is very normal to be afraid. There are a lot of unknowns and you feel like you have no control over what is going on around you. Everyone feels fear to some degree.

It's okay to be angry, as long as you don't hurt anyone or break anything when you are.

> True – it is a very normal reaction to be angry. Be very careful how you express your anger though.

Jesus was never angry.

> False – In Mark 11 the Bible tells a story when Jesus came into the temple area and they were selling goods. He got angry and overturned the tables and made them leave. This is a great example of it being okay to express your anger when justified, but being careful how you express it.

Teens that can identify their feelings and express them in good ways are healthier than those who don't express their feelings.

> True – One of the most healthiest things you can do during this time is to accept and express whatever feelings you are having.

FALSE

TRUE

True or False Questions

Anger is a sin.

> False – It is not a sin to feel angry. It is what you do with your anger that usually turns out to be a sin.

It is possible to have too many emotions.

> False – Everyone and every situation is different. No one should be judged according to their own situations. Everyone's situation is different.

Every single feeling is important.

> True – There is no feeling that is unimportant and all feelings need to be shared.

It's best to cry when you are alone.

> False – It may be easier to cry when you are alone but you should not feel like that is the only time you can cry. Crying is not something that needs be done only in private.

Good kids are always happy.

> False – Whether you are happy or not does not determine whether you are good or not.

When you are upset with someone the best thing for you to do is to keep quiet.

> False – It is not healthy for you to stuff your feelings. Depending on the situation it may not be best to talk directly to the person you are upset at but it would be good to talk it over with someone you can trust.

Hating something or someone is okay and normal.

> False – We are never suppose to hate anything. When you feel hate, you become bitter thus making it very hard to forgive. God has called each one of us to forgive as He has forgiven us.

You always need a reason to be sad or upset.

> False – sometimes you don't even know what your reason is. It is through going to groups like this that help you define your reason.

Not talking to someone is a way of solving a problem.

> False – By not talking to someone you are ignoring the situation not solving it.

Things would be better if you were perfect.

> False – Feeling this way is not reality. We live in a fallen world and no one is perfect. We need to learn to live within our failures and shortcomings in order to learn what God is teaching us.

I am always responsible for my actions.

> True – Each one of us are responsible for our actions. Someone else may be responsible for the situation that has made you react but how you react is totally your responsibility.

With enough hard work, I can fix anything.

> False – You can fix only that which you have control over. No matter how hard you may try to fix your parents marriage or relationship, you do not have any control over that. What you do have control over is yourself. With hard work you can get through this and take steps to prevent it happening in your life in the future.

True or False Questions

My life is my life and no one knows me better than me, so no one can give me advice.

False – although you may think you know yourself better than anybody else, another person who you can trust can often times give you an objective opinion on things in your life that you have never seen before. Getting someone else's opinion is always a good idea, as long as you know that they care about you and you can trust their opinion.

I am considered weak if I ask for help.

False – Everyone needs help every now and then. God has given us the need for others in our lives. We need to allow others to help us when we are in need.

Anger is fine if you can control it.

True – Anger is not a sin, it is what you do with anger that turns it into sin.

God has given each of us an incredible number of feelings. Some of them are fun and we like to feel them, and others are scary and difficult and we will do anything we can to keep from feeling them.

True – As hard as it is to acknowledge your feelings and deal with them, it is only by doing this that you can move on and make changes for your future.

TRUE

TRUE

FALSE

FALSE

Twister Mixer

1. If your parents are currently separated, place your left hand on blue.
2. If you have a little brother, place your left foot on red.
3. If you have a step mom, place your right foot on green.
4. If you have a little sister, place your right hand on yellow.
5. If you have a big brother, place your left hand on red.
6. If you have a step dad, place your left foot on blue.
7. If your parents are divorced, place your right foot on blue.
8. If your parents have been divorced for over 3 years, put your right hand on red.
9. If you have a step sister, place your left hand on red.
10. If your dad lives out of the state, place your left foot on green.
11. If you had to move because of the divorce, place your right foot on yellow.
12. If you had to change schools because of the divorce, place your right hand on blue.
13. If your parents are still living in the same home, place your left foot on blue.
14. If you have a half brother, place your left foot on yellow.
15. If you live mostly with your mom, place your right foot on red.
16. If you have a step brother, place your right hand on green.
17. If you have a big sister, place your left hand on green.
18. If you have a pet dog, place your left foot on blue.
19. If you have 8 sets of grandparents, place your right foot on yellow.
20. If you have a big sister, place your right hand on blue.
21. If you have a pet cat, place your left hand on yellow.
22. If you have had to move to a different town, place your left foot on green.
23. If you go to your dads every other weekend, place your right foot on red.
24. If you live mostly with your dad, place your right hand on blue.
25. If your mom has moved out of state, place your left hand on red.
26. If you dad lives more than 2 hours away, place your right foot on blue.
27. If you are seeing a counselor, place your right hand on yellow.
28. If your mom has remarried, place your left foot on blue.
29. If your dad has remarried, place your right foot on green.
30. If you have a best friend, place your left hand on blue.
31. If you don't see your dad, place your left foot on red.
32. If you don't see your mom, place your right foot on yellow.
33. If you hate divorce, place your right hand on yellow.
34. If you are angry, place your left hand on green.
35. If you stay with your parents equal time, place your right foot on red.

Wheel Of Fortune Phrases

Week One – There Are No Perfect Families

Week Two – The Slippery Slope

Week Three – Getting A Grip

Week Four – It's Not My Fault

Week Five – Who Knows You Baby?

Week Six – Where Is God When It Hurts?

Week Seven – All My Feelings Are Okay

Week Eight – Now What Do I Do?

Week Nine – The Bumpy Road

Week Ten – What's The Real Deal?

Week Eleven – Moving On and Letting Go

Week Twelve – Beauty From Ashes

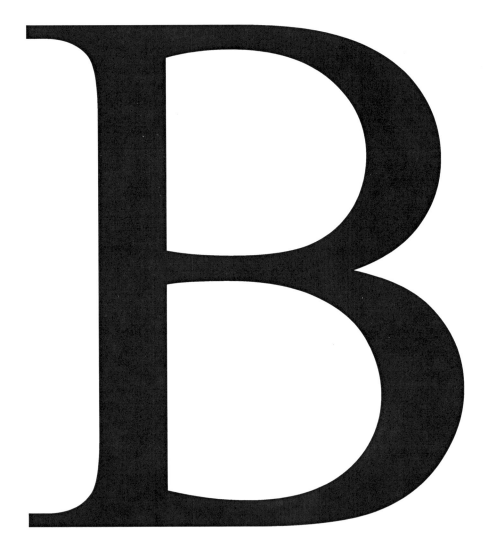

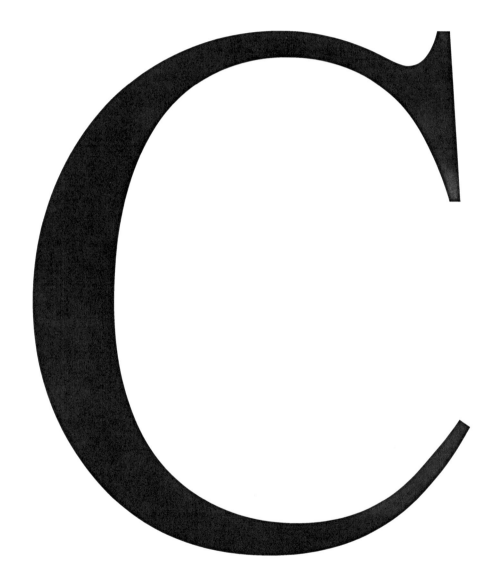

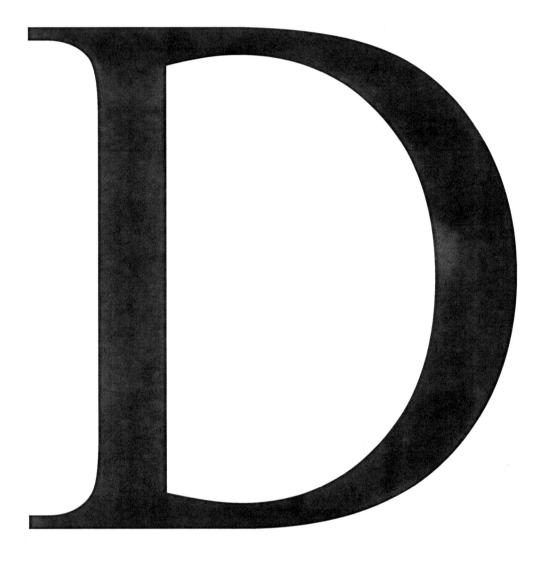

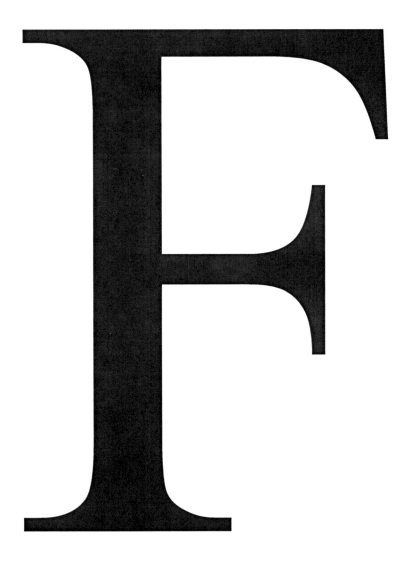

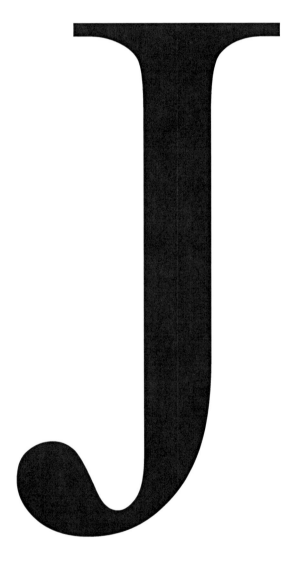

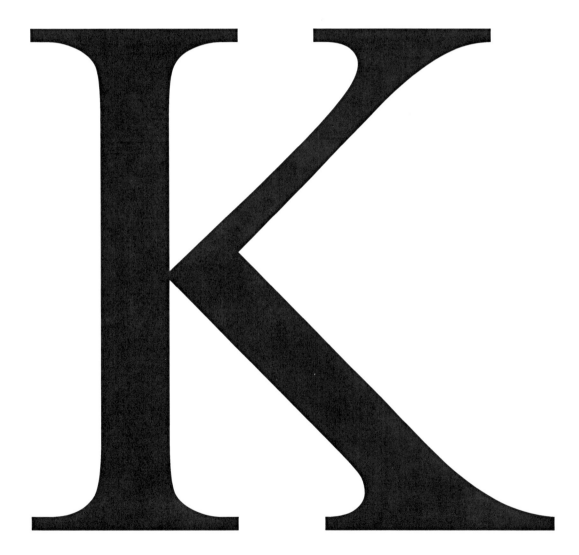

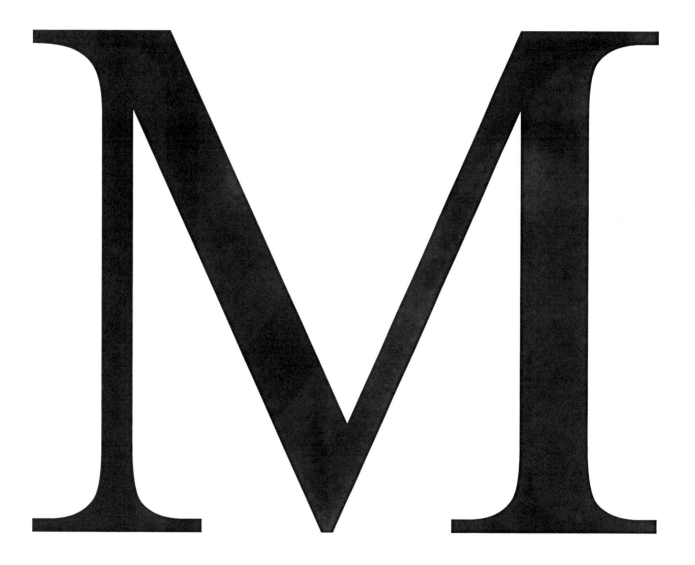

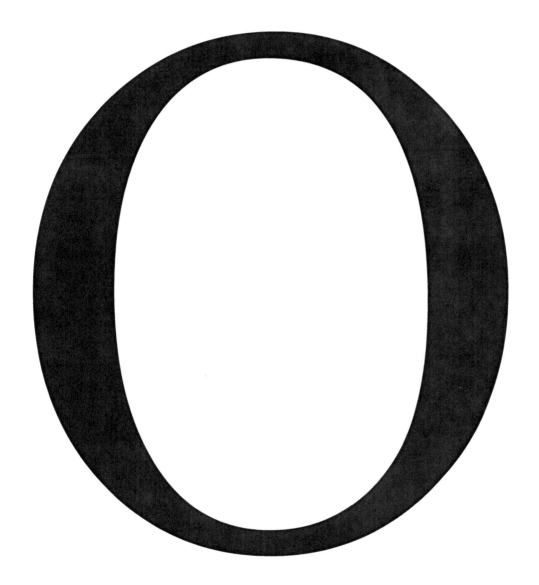

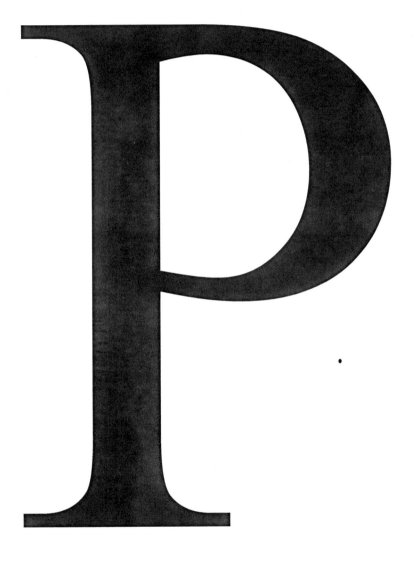

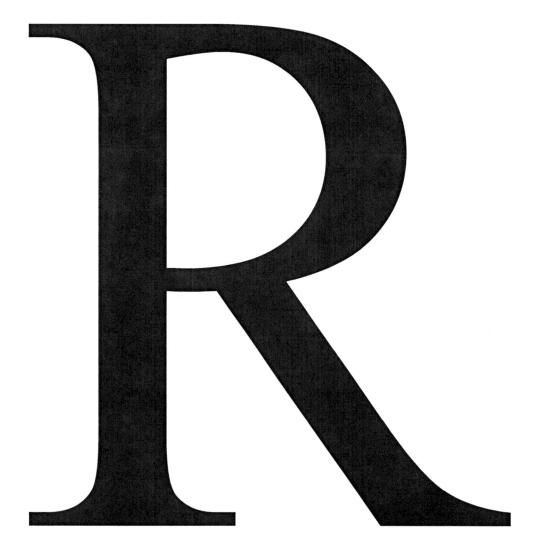

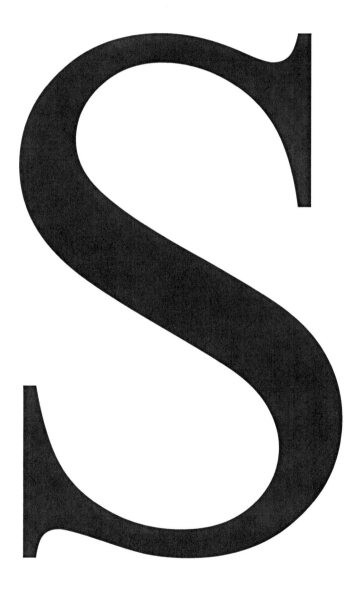

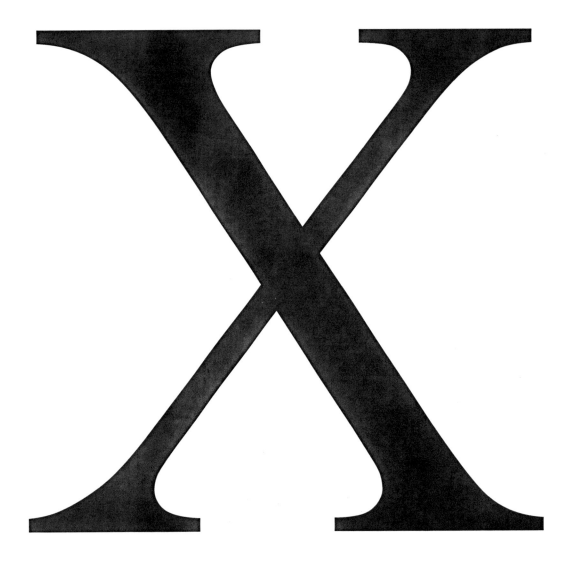

The creator of THE BIG D brings you another great tool to be used in your groups....

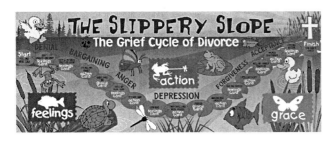

ONE NEW GAME
3 GREAT FORMATS!

KIDS JUMP FROM LILY PAD TO LILY PAD AND DISCOVER THE SECRET TO OVERCOMING THE HURTS OF THE GRIEF CYCLE.

RIDE THE ROLLER COASTER OF EMOTIONS AND FEEL THE THRILL OF FINISHING A WINNER.

SPECIFICALLY DESIGNED FOR ADULTS EXPERIENCING A SEPARATION OR DIVORCE. A GREAT TOOL TO USE AS AN ICE BREAKER FOR YOUR RECOVERY GROUPS.

This is your ticket to jump on board and explore the SLIPPERY SLOPE.

On the SLIPPERY SLOPE are the feelings we all experience when going through separation or divorce.

Whether you are working with young children, teenagers, or adults we have a game to meet your needs. Explore the feelings of denial, anger, depression, forgiveness and more. We've created three unique formats to meet the needs of each specific age group.

The SLIPPERY SLOPE will help guide you through the emotional process of grief while sharing the grace, forgiveness and love of Christ.

ORDER YOUR TODAY! $39.95 PER GAME OR $99.95 FOR ALL THREE GAMES.

To order additional copies of

Divorce Thru the Eyes of a Teen

Activity Guide

contact AMFM Press by

phone at

(480) 585-0109

or

on the Internet at

www.amfmpress.com

or go to

Sonset Point Ministries at

www.sonsetpointministries.com

To view more information or order online direct

Breinigsville, PA USA
02 August 2010
242784BV00003B/1/P

9 780979 662034